Harken:

A knowledgeable marketer will make a few bucks, but the wise marketer will make a fortune.

What is wisdom?

Well, using email marketing as context, let me explain it this way:

Knowledge is knowing that subject lines with all capitals get attention. Wisdom is knowing not to use all capitals in your subject lines.

The reason is that using all capitals will only get you negative attention.

You follow?

Now, hear this:

The saddest aspect of the advertising industry right now is that the industry gathers knowledge faster than marketers can gather wisdom. And, knowledge without wisdom is about as useless as a senior citizen with an iPad.

Thus, this little book is wisdom focused.

Yes, dear reader, this book is not designed to just stuff your head full of information (although there's plenty of that too) but rather stuff it full of wisdom.

I'm talking about the ability to take the sales information in this book (and the sales information you already have between your ears) and turn it into dollars.

That's right . . . sales!

Although this book has a strong focus on email marketing, the wisdom therein transcends email marketing.

Not only will this wisdom help you make a bundle of money selling your wares, but it will make you a more persuasive and influential individual, which of course, will affect everything you do.

Oh yeah, one last thing.

Don't expect any significant, lengthy intros (or any length) with these chapters.

You'll see what I mean after the first few.

Contents

kelvindorsey.com

George Lucas

T he secret to sales is also an illusion.

The assumption is that great salespeople fill their prospects with a desire to buy their wares.

Nope.

Not true.

People already have desires.

Listen: You cannot fill someone with a desire any more than you can fill Snoop Dog's house full of anti-marijuana posters.

It ain't gonna happen, homie.

Verily I say, Bill Cosby has more chance of filling up a woman's wine glass at a bar than you do filling someone with desire.

Do you hear what I'm saying?

You cannot "create" desire.

Either someone has it, or they don't.

Know this:

Your first job as a marketer is to find a group of people who *ALREADY* have a desire that your product or service fulfills.

Your second job is this:

To take this group's desire and direct it, channel it, and focus it on your product or service.

Listen, no marketer has ever filled a female prospect with the desire to feel thin and beautiful. But many a marketer has shown a female prospect how their product or service can make them thin and beautiful.

Capisce?

Molto bene.

Hey, that was a neat little lesson, wasn't it?

I'm glad you agree.

Now, normally this is where I do a clever little segue into promoting my product.

But not today.

Why?

Cuz I can't think of one, OK?

"The best and most beautiful things in the world cannot be seen or even touched — they must be felt with the heart."

Helen Keller

K now this:

People believe what they want to believe.

Everybody looks through their own belief filter.

This belief filter blocks out any information or facts that directly oppose a person's belief and locates all information and facts that support their belief. (You should reread that paragraph.)

As a marketer, if you say something that contradicts your market's core belief, it's game over.

You must keep in line with your marketer's core beliefs.

However, that's not enough.

You see, your prospects want to believe your sales pitch. They want your product or service to do what you say it will do because, ultimately, they will benefit from it. But if you don't give them supporting facts and proof, they won't pull out their hard earned.

And if you want your prospects to be more willing to accept and believe your facts and proof, then . . . you must stomp on your prospect's greed glands.

Yep, you gotta make them frothing at the mouth excited about your product or service.

You see, when folk get emotionally involved with an idea, they will seek out information to confirm and justify their idea or belief.

What I'm trying to say here is this:

The heart tells the head what to believe.

Most marketers get that backasswards.

They direct their pitch to a prospect's logical mind. But that's like telling a four-year-old to eat their veggies because of all the nutritional vitamins their body will benefit from.

They don't care!

They will only care if you give them a reason to care, like, for example:

"Hey Kiddo, if you eat these beans and carrots you can stay up later tonight." Ah, now that child is emotionally involved with the idea of eating those veggies, right? And, they will now be open to learning about the logical reason for eating vegetables.

When the heart is engaged, we become open and suggestive to any logic or facts that support the thing our heart secretly desires.

Verily I say unto thee . . .

Your emails should be felt with the heart above all things.

It's all about the heart.

Even Helen Keller could see that!

"Yes, I believe blue material is funny, but if that's all you've got, you're dead in the water."

Howard Stern

I'll admit, I push the boundaries with similes and humor in my emails, but upon closer inspection, you will find my emails all contain a valuable piece of information therein, that if applied, will help make you more sales.

Listen, your subscribers signed up to *your* newsletter cuz they have some problem they want resolved.

So yes, make your emails entertaining, by all means, but make damn sure they also help solve the main problem your subscribers are looking for you to help solve.

Comprendo?

Good.

Hey, there were two Howard Stern quotes I just couldn't choose between. So I'm gonna give you both.

Here's the second to finish off:

"I'm pretty sure that if you know what candy crush is you're a loser."

Agreed.

"A good hockey player plays where the puck is. A great hockey player plays where the puck is going to be."

Wayne Gretzky

A good email marketer will address a subscriber's objection *if* a subscriber contacts them.

A great email marketer answers a subscriber's objection *before* a subscriber contacts them.

See the difference?

In sport, what separates the great athletes from the good athletes is anticipation.

And the same holds true for email marketing.

The marketer who can anticipate his subscriber's objections will always be ahead of the game.

It comes down to acting vs. reacting.

Waiting for a subscriber to contact you before answering an objection is like a hockey player waiting for the puck to come their way . . . it's a terrible strategy.

You're always gonna be a dollar short and a day late.

Look, I've always said that the best emails you can send your subscribers are emails that answer and overcome a common objection that your prospects have about your product or service.

Heed this advice, and you'll start seeing sales pour in like a crowd of Canadians at a Waffle House opening.

"A lot of singers think all they have to do is exercise their tonsils to get ahead. They refuse to look for new ideas and new outlets, so they fall by the wayside. I'm going to try to find out the new ideas before the others do."

Ella Fitzgerald

Y ou know, a lot of email marketers think all they have to do is learn copywriting to get ahead.

But that's like a woman relying on her looks instead of working on herself (i.e., her personality, communication skills, mindset and personal disciplines).

In other words, she's compromising and settling for okay, instead of great.

Sure, if she's good looking enough, she will get by, but she will most likely attract douchebags who either just wanna get in her pants, or have her as a trophy wife.

Listen, the same holds true for email marketing.

Sure, if your copywriting chops are good, you'll get by, but if you truly want your marketing results to be great, you're gonna need . . .

. . . New Ideas!

It ain't enough to be a good writer or copywriter, Bubba.

Because the truth is, your writing or copywriting is only as good as your big idea (new idea).

It's a new idea, new angle, or new approach that makes your copywriting work, just like hit songs are the results of good songs— not good singers.

Consider this:

There are only 12 notes in all of music, yet the great songwriters come up with a new and fresh combination of those 12 notes that will resonate with a huge audience.

And so it is with promoting a product or service. There are only a handful of benefits for any product or service, right?

Yet the great marketer comes up with a new and fresh way to communicate or present those benefits.

You see, if you are focused on coming up with new ideas and not just focusing on your writing, it won't matter in the slightest if all your competitors are talking about the same product benefits as you.

Why?

Because YOU will be communicating those benefits in a new, fresh, and original way.

Listen: Let your incestual competition copy each other.

Let them talk about product or service benefits the in same ole, same ole way.

Let them parrot your industries sales jargon, slogans, and taglines.

Let them have no point of difference.

Let them become a commodity.

Just make damn sure YOU are always coming up with new ways to communicate your benefits.

Let me give you an example of coming up with a new way to present a common or industry shared benefit.

A list copywriter Parris Lampropoulos who writes sales letters for Bottom Line Inc. (American newsletter publishing company) had the challenge of writing a sales letter for one of Bottom Line's financial products.

This was an information product that centered around the wisdom of Warren Buffet. So, essentially, the product's benefit is that you're getting the very best expert advice. However, Parris, being the smart individual he is, knew he would have to come up with a new way to communicate that benefit.

Simply because every copywriter, blogger, and journalist has flogged the "Warren Buffet's secrets" headline within an inch of its life.

People read a headline such as Warren Buffet's Secrets For The Stock Market, or whatever, and they think, Yeah, I've read Warren's Autobiography and his other books on investing. Nah, it's probably nothing I haven't read or heard before.

And more likely than not, they totally dismiss it.

But Parris Lampropoulos doesn't accept people dismissing his sales copy.

No siree.

So, Parris hunkered down in his office and started reading through his research papers like a fiend. He was looking for that one big idea that would allow him to present his benefit (Warren Buffet's advice on investing) in a new way.

Well, as he was going through his papers, he came across a Warren Buffet quote that read: "I don't worry about the gloom and doom stuff, I buy companies that survive."

This reminded Parris of a joke he read in People Magazine just days earlier.

That joke was this:

If there were a nuclear holocaust, the only thing that would survive is cockroaches and Keith Richards.

Well, Parris's cunning little mind started connecting the dots.

"Great googley moogley, I've got it!" said Parris.

He then grabbed his notepad and scribbled down his "new idea" headline.

And, here is what he scribbled on his notepad:

Never Before Revealed . . .
Warren Buffett's "Cockroach Strategy"
For Getting Rich In The Stock Market

Now, how well did that headline work for Bottom Line Inc.?

It worked like a charm!

That became the new control (the best performing sales copy).

It truly teased their market's curiosity and tickled their greed glands mercilessly.

You see, when the market read that headline, they were thinking, "Hmm, haven't heard that one before. Oh goodie, this is something new!"

And that my friend, is what it takes. It takes a spanking new idea to capture your market's imagination and attention.

When you start communicating your product or service in a new way . . .

. . . your sales will multiply quicker than a Catholic rabbit.

www.kelvindorsey.com

Roald Dahl

S top and think of something in your life right now that is kinda upsetting you.

Maybe you just fought with your spouse or partner?

Perhaps your child is acting the fool?

Maybe your bills are piling up, and you don't know if you're gonna make rent or payroll?

Or maybe your long-time pet just died.

I bet you have thought of something, right?

Well, guess what, you are not alone.

We all have something in our life, right this moment, upsetting us on some level.

And so it is with your subscribers.

They too, have some issue going on in their lives.

Now listen:

Life, like this story, can get a little too serious sometimes, and we need to lighten the load.

And if you can do that in some small way for your subscribers, you will become a welcome guest in their inbox instead of just another pesky email marketer looking to crawl into their wallets.

So, how do we go about lightening our subscriber's load and brightening up their day?

Easy.

By not being as serious as a mortician . . . even if you're a mortician!

In other words: Lighten the hell up!

Stop being so "professional" (boring) and don't be so afraid of acting the fool now and then.

I don't care if you're selling a product or service to cancer patients, in fact, cancer patients will appreciate it even more.

Sure, take your marketing seriously, but every now and then, throw in a little nonsense.

Your subscribers will cherish it.

And those subscribers who don't?

Well, they can unsubscribe their sorry-asses.

That's right, show 'em the unsubscribe button.

"If you have a great band with a mediocre drummer, you have a mediocre band. If you have a mediocre band with a great drummer, you have a great band!"

Duke Ellington

K now this:

If you have a mediocre list of subscribers (i.e., they are not very qualified) with a great email marketer, you will get a mediocre response.

If you have a great list of subscribers (i.e., they are highly qualified) with a mediocre email marketer, you will get a great response.

Listen, dude, if you really wanna get your marketing campaigns to swing, then focus on building a more targeted list of subscribers. That's right; it's the quality of your list that will make or break your email campaign.

Get that part wrong, nothing will work.

But get it right, then everything else becomes infinitely easier.

But Kelvin, what about copywriting?

What about it?

The best copywriter in the world cannot sell to a list of unqualified subscribers.

It's the same with your offer.

I don't care how good your deal is, if your list of subscribers don't want it, it's not gonna jive.

Maybe this will help you.

Your list of subscribers will determine 50% of your response.

Your offer will determine 30% of your response.

Your sales copy will determine 20% of your response.

Yup, it's your list of subscribers that will make or break you.

And just like a great drummer keeps the groove going, a great list of subscribers will keep the gravy train coming.

"A woman can be very beautiful and an ideal model, and she will photograph incredibly well, but she'll appear in film, and it won't work. What works is some fusion of physical beauty with some mental field or whatever you call it. I don't know."

Oliver Stone

A nd so it is with email.

You can take a brilliant writer who leaves a gasping, select audience (English and literary teachers) in awe with every sparking gem of crafted prose and get them writing promotional emails, and the email campaign will be a complete flop.

Why is it so?

I'll tell you why.

Because email marketing is not about writing.

Nope.

Email marketing is about salesmanship.

And salesmanship 101 is this:

Get your prospect to know, like, and trust you.

Thus, WHAT you write is more important than HOW you write.

Harken,

Ask thyself the following three questions:

(1) What am I writing that will help my subscribers get to know me?

(2) What am I writing that will get my subscribers to like me?

(3) What am I writing that will get my subscribers to trust me?

Listen:

You could write all your promotional emails with the literary brilliance of Charles Dickens, but if *what* you write doesn't get your subscribers to know, like, and trust you, you may as well sign off as a Nigerian Prince then ask them to send you ten thousand dollars.

Either way, you're not getting a response.

But if you heed my advice and start writing your emails with those three questions in mind, your subscribers will open up to you like a client on a psychiatrist's couch.

But Kelvin, I don't want my subscribers to open up, I want their wallets to open up.

Listen,

I have just told you how to get them to open their wallets.

I guess I have to spell it out for you, huh?

If you want to open up your subscriber's wallets, you must first open up their minds and hearts.

End of lesson.

*"I knew I was a winner back in the late sixties.
I knew I was destined for great things. People
will say that kind of thinking is totally immodest.
I agree. Modesty is not a word that applies to me
in any way — I hope it never will."*

Arnold Schwarzenegger

M odesty might be a good quality to have as an individual, but as a marketer, it's the kiss of death.

Being modest in your marketing will leave you broker than the tooth fairy at a house full of meth addicts.

You see, "modesty" is the very antithesis of marketing.

If you're guilty of being "modest" in your promotional emails, well, just knock it off, okay?

It ain't cool, and it sure as hell ain't profitable.

But Kelvin, I don't want to come across as showy, boastful, or arrogant.

Look, let me ask you something. Do you have a product or service you're proud of and will help your subscribers?

You do?

Well, do you think you're doing right by your subscribers by <u>not</u> doing everything in your powers of persuasion to get your product or service into their hands?

Listen, if you don't start crowing, boasting, bragging, and proudly promoting your product or service, two things will happen:

(1) Your subscribers won't believe in your product or service (if *you* don't, why should they?) and therefore won't buy.

(2) Your subscribers won't get the help that only *you* can offer them.

And that my friend, is a real soup sandwich.

Ok, the bottom line is this:

If you want to bag more sales, you'd better get braggin'.

You know, out of all the brilliant marketing lessons I've taught you, I think this lesson may well be one of my very best.

I tell ya, it's hard to be modest when you're this damn good.

*"The worst thing I can be is the same
as everybody else. I hate that."*

Arnold Schwarzenegger

I n the world of advertising, if you're not different, you're dead in the water, the street, the web, and wherever else you're trying to get noticed.

Being the same as everyone else in your market makes you about as relevant as Myspace and Hammer Pants.

But know this: You, me, and everyone else ARE different.

There's not one individual on the spinning ball we inhabit that isn't unique.

Then why is it so hard to differentiate between businesses and brands?

It's simple.

People are copycats.

Would you like to hear Dr. Kelvin's explanation for why us humans copy each other?

And no, I'm not going to parrot the evolutionary psychologists who wax lyrical about this copycat phenomenon coming from when we used to run around with spears and live in tribes. You know, that safety in numbers thing they love to talk about?

Look, that may well be true, but let's get real for a moment.

The real reason why business owners copy other businesses in their industry is because they lack confidence in themselves.

I tell you, the average business owner is so timid they make *The Cowardly Lion* look like *Aslan*.

The average biz owner just don't back themselves.

They're timider than a hotel clerk serving Russel Crowe.

They see their quirks, foibles, and oddities as a weakness instead of a point of difference that can be exploited.

Arnold Schwarzenegger was told again and again by movie producers that he would never make it as a leading actor because he was too big (literally), he could barely speak English, and his name was too long.

But you can't stop a man who has vision, determination, and who backs himself.

And as we all know now, Arnie's "weaknesses" became his greatest strengths.

His seemingly lack of Hollywood attributes was what finally made him the stand-out amongst the rest of male Hollywood actors.

And that my friend, is half the battle.

Listen, if you don't stand out in your industry, you'll always struggle for attention. Thus, you won't get mentioned. You'll probably end up on the pension, and that will cause hypertension. I'm sorry, I get caught up in rhymes sometimes. (Can you tell I've been listening to a lot of Eminem lately?)

In marketing, not being different brings indifference. (I shoulda been a rappa.)

And if your subscribers are indifferent towards you, well, it's like trying to have a conversation with a coma patient—there will be little to no response.

You know, few of my subscribers are indifferent towards me.

My subscribers either hate me or love me.

And that equates to a highly responsive list.

However, you need to embrace your uniqueness and sell with confidence.

Selling with confidence makes all the difference.

It's the difference between Walmart and a lemonade stand.

Very truly I say unto you, those who grab the brass ring in life are those who are bold as brass.

Hey, Kelvin, my list seems very unresponsive, what do you recommend?

Well, in the words of Arnie, stop being a big girlie man, and start marketing like the man or woman you are.

www.kelvindorsey.com

"When I heard Aretha, I could feel her emotional delivery so clearly. It came from down deep within. That's what I wanted to do."

Whitney Houston

Y ou know, that's what is missing in most people's promotional emails.

There's no freakin' emotion!

No heart or soul.

Nuttin'.

Just empty words void of all personality, feeling, and emotion.

Sorry, Sweetcakes, that's not gonna cut it.

A piece of content (no matter what the medium) that lacks emotion will lack engagement.

Why is it you can sit through a two-hour movie while it's a struggle to read a two-minute promotional email?

It's simple.

It's all about emotion.

A movie stirs your emotions.

Promotional emails don't.

I told you it was simple.

Listen, sending a promotional email that contains no emotion and expecting a response is like expecting Floyd Mayweather to fight without offering him millions of dollars —it ain't gonna happen.

Listen, if you want to get some response from your promotional emails, you can't just "phone it in."

No, you need passion. Enthusiasm. Sincerity. You must have an opinion and state that opinion in no uncertain terms.

Yup, you need to say what you mean and mean what you say.

Will you get some haters?

Sure.

But guess what?

You'll also get fans.

I'm sorry, but you can't get fans without picking up some haters along the way.

Show me a marketer who has no haters, and I'll show you a marketer who has no fans.

"I used to be embarrassed because I was just a comic book writer while other people were building bridges or going on to medical careers. And then I began to realize: Entertainment is one of the most important things in people's lives. Without it they might go off the deep end. I feel that if you're able to entertain people, you're doing a good thing."

Stan Lee

Y es, I agree, Mr. Lee, entertainment is valuable in and of itself.

And while I'm a big advocate of giving value in the form of information, I'm an even bigger fan of giving away value in the form of entertainment.

Look, I can't say it any better than Stan Lee, so I'm not even gonna try.

Just read Stan Lee's quote again, and take heed.

But be ready because . . .

. . . With great entertainment comes great response.

Did that sound hokey to you?

I guess it does.

But that doesn't mean it ain't true.

*"I don't believe in psychology.
I believe in good moves."*

Bobby Fisher

I don't believe in copywriting. I believe in good products.

Do you know how hard it is to promote a crappy product or service?

Let me put it in copywriting terms: Do you know how many lies you will have to tell? (That's a joke, Silly.)

Listen, coming up with good sales copy for a lousy product or service is like coming up with a compliment for an ugly person with bad dress sense.

On the other hand, if you have a great product or service, the sales copy almost writes itself.

As Gary Bencivenga (if you don't know who he is, you should) pointed out, "A gifted product is greater than a gifted pen."

Think of it this way:

The product or service is the horse, and the copywriter is the jockey. The best jockey in the world can't win a race on a horse that's a complete duffer and runs like a camel.

The bottom line is this:

The greatest advantage you can have in business is a great product or service.

Amen.

"It's just rock and roll. A lot of times we get criticized for it. A lot of music papers come out with: 'When are they going to stop playing these three chords?' If you believe you shouldn't play just three chords it's pretty silly on their part. To us, the simpler a song is, the better, 'cause it's more in line with what the person on the street is."

Angus Young

A h yes, simplicity.

It's a beautiful word, isn't it?

I mean, it rolls nicely off the tongue and has a sweet sound to it too.

Well anyways, let's talk about simplicity for a moment.

I'm a big fan of simplicity. I try to make everything I do more simple. If I can't make something simpler, I either outsource it or drop it like a bad habit.

And when it comes to writing sales copy, I'm even more aggressive in my simplification.

In fact, my whole approach to sales copy is the equivalent of a three-chord pop song.

I'll show you.

Here are my three copywriting power chords:

(1) Here's what I've got.

(2) Here's what it'll do for you, and . . .

(3) Here's how to get it.

You likey?

"You gotta believe in yourself.
Hell, I believe I'm the best-looking
guy in the world and I might be right!"

Charles Barkley

K elvin's take:

They say in sport, 'confidence' is everything.

Well, guess what, my little marketing crony?

The same can be said for email.

Before your subscribers can believe in your product's benefits, they first must believe in YOU.

And if you don't believe in you, your subscribers NEVER will!

So . . .

. . . sack-up and . . .

. . . Believe In Yourself!

Peace.

*"I used to have a drug problem,
now I make enough money."*

David Lee Roth

Kelvin's elucidation:

A wise man once said . . .

"Money solves the problems that not having enough money creates." (Think it over.)

Now, I don't care who you are, we <u>all</u> have certain problems caused by a lack of the green stuff.

You do.

I do.

Even the great philanthropic Bill Gates could do more good through his charitable foundation with more moolah.

But as email marketers, we can solve our problems (caused by a dollar deficiency) by doing these two things:

(1) Keep building your list

(2) Keep improving your salesmanship

Well . . .

. . . don't just sit there. . . go do those two things . . .

. . . **EVERY. SINGLE. DAY.**

And all will be well—eventually (I hate that part!)

Peace.

"I fear not the man who has practiced 10,000 kicks once, but I fear the man who has practiced one kick 10,000 times."

Bruce Lee

Kelvin's elucidation:

I fear not the marketer who knows a little about . . .

Social Media marketing, Twitter, Facebook ads, YouTube, content marketing, Pinterest, SEO, and List Building, but, I fear the marketer who has mastered Direct Response Marketing.

Most marketer's focus is more stretched than the elastic in Nicki Minaj's underwear.

Focusing on too many things will just make you mediocre at a lot of things.

That's boo how (not good).

Listen, Grasshopper . . .

It's much better to master one thing.

And as an email marketer, there is no more powerful a thing you can do for your business than to master Direct Response Marketing.

If I were you, I'd get on it like white on rice!

Zai jian.

*"It's mind-altering when you slip into someone
else's shoes. That's psychedelic, man."*

Bryan Cranston

Kelvin's Elucidation:

T here's no denying that a major factor in Breaking Bad's success
is Bryan Cranston's *chillingly* good acting in playing Walter
White.

A great actor like Bryan Cranston has mastered the ability to put
himself entirely into the shoes of another person.

Bryan completely disassociated himself and inhabited someone
else's identity—Walter White.

To the degree that an actor does this, is the degree of success they
will have in giving an authentic and powerful performance.

And to the degree an audience will "buy it."

And email marketing is no different to acting.

How?

Just trust me, okay?

Alright, alright, if you *must* know, here's how:

To the degree a marketer puts themselves in their customer's shoes,
is the degree of success they will have in giving an authentic and
powerful sales pitch.

And to the degree your customers will buy!

Kelvin Dorsey ~ Email Marketing Maverick

Say my name.

Email Marketing Maverick.

You're damn right it is.

On David Beckham:

"He cannot kick with his left foot, he cannot head a ball, he cannot tackle and he doesn't score many goals. Apart from that he's alright."

George Best

M ost email marketers can barely get their emails opened, they can't get their subscribers attention, they can't write a compelling sales pitch, and they don't get many sales.

Apart from that, they're alright.

Is there a lesson here?

YES.

Don't be one of them!

"At home I am a nice guy: but I don't want the world to know. Humble people, I've found, don't get very far."

Muhammad Ali

B eing "humble" in your email promotions is a sure-fire way to go broke.

The only "sale" you'll make being humble is selling your subscribers on the idea that your product or service is not for them.

If you want sales, you must first get your subscriber's attention, then you must persuade them.

How?

By bragging about your product or service.

You must boast, gloat, and crow!

Huh?

You don't like to brag, you say?

Well, let me reply to that, with another Ali quote:

"It ain't braggin' if you can back it up."

Let me ask you this:

Does your product or service back up your claims?

You say it does?

Then wherefore do thou act like such a pussy?

Look, if you wanna make more sales with your email marketing, then memorize this:

To Get Your Subscribers Vote, You Gotta Showboat and Gloat!

(That was such a good little rhyme I bet you thought that was Ali's, eh?)

Whatever.

Ding, ding!

Hey, looks like this round goes to yours truly.

"Knowledge speaks,
but wisdom listens."

Jimmy Hendrix

W hen it comes to "making the sale," it's not <u>how much</u> you know that counts, it's <u>what</u> you know that counts.

Harken:

A good salesman will shut his pie-hole and open his ear holes.

He does this cuz he knows if he lets his prospect talk, more often than not, his prospects will sell themselves.

He also knows that by keeping quiet and listening, he'll discover the two things about his prospect that will almost guarantee the sale.

What are those two things?

Simply this:

(1) Their main concerns and problems.

(2) The way they talk.

Hear this:

Once you know those two things about your prospect, well, you've almost got the sale in the bag.

All that's left, my friend, is to deliver your sales pitch.

You do that by simply talking (in their particular vernacular) to them about their biggest problem then offering to solve it by way of your service or product.

The takeaway:

Keep the hole in your trachea closed, until the holes on either side of your head have done their job.

Class dismissed.

But Kelvin, you didn't show me how all this translates into email marketing?

Listen . . .

. . . If you can't translate all this to your email marketing, then you have more serious problems than . . .

. . . ahh, forget it!

Kelvin Dorsey

Helping smart marketers (and a few morons) around the world with their email marketing.

"I've outdone anyone you can name — Mozart, Beethoven, Bach, Strauss. Irving Berlin, he wrote 1,001 tunes. I wrote 5,500."

James Brown

The Maverick's elucidation:

They didn't call him the hardest working man in show business for no reason.

When it came to working, James Brown worked harder than a cat burying a turd on a marble floor.

Imagine the schedule of a presidential candidate in mid-campaign. Now imagine keeping that schedule for 30 years straight with no breaks.

That was James Brown.

Now, hear this:

If you take a peek behind the closed doors of someone who's dominating an industry, sport or whatever, and closely observe them, do you know what you'll see?

Here's what you'll see:

An almost sickening work ethic that will shock you to your very core.

And, they don't work hard because they're the best, they're the best because they work hard.

This also holds true for email marketing.

You see, an email marketer without a James Brown-esque work ethic will be left as frustrated as an Amish electrician, and just as broke.

In this game, if you ain't got work ethic, you should get the funk out!

But for the folk who have stopped looking for secrets, shortcuts or any other fairy tale road to success, and have embraced the grind, well, they've already won.

They may not have collected their prize yet, but it's coming!

Hoo Hah!

I feel good.

All this talk of hard work has me all excited.

Oh, one last, but very important point to remember:

Work hard, but always, and I mean always, keep it funky!

*"My greatest strength is that
I have no weaknesses."*

John McEnroe

E mail marketing is just like any other solo sport.
You can't rely on anyone but yourself.

If you win, it's on you.

If you lose, it's on you.

And if you have any weakness, you'll be left as vulnerable as a cat walking around a Korean restaurant at dinner time.

In tennis, if your opponent notices you're a little shaky on your backhand, he'll exploit that all day long.

Listen, any tennis player who's ever made it to number one in the world has eliminated all weaknesses and therefore, more times than not, they win.

In tennis, there are many things to master, such as:

Footwork, defense, backhands, forehands, serving, volleys, fitness, mindset, strategy, tactics, and technique.

What about email marketing?

What must an email marketer master?

Here's what:

Copywriting, marketing (lead generation), writing, and storytelling.

And just like in tennis, if your competition senses any weakness in your game, they will exploit it.

That's right, Champ; they aren't gonna ask your permission to take your market share; they'll just take it like a fat kid near a piece of chocolate cake.

Hey, what did you think of today's lesson?

Huh?

Just ok?

YOU CANNOT BE SERIOUS!

"Rock and Roll music, if you like it, if you feel it, you can't help but move to it."

Elvis Presley

M usic and email marketing?
Can they be compared?

You betcha sweet lil pippy.

Music is an emotional experience.

And guess what?

So is selling.

Listen, if you don't have a deep understanding that selling is an emotional transaction, you'll forever be a day late and a dollar short.

Know this:

People buy with their emotions and only use logic to answer someone who wants to know why they bought it. (Buy with emotion—justify with logic.)

You see, a guy will emotionally buy the new Callaway golf clubs to make HIMSELF happy.

Then he'll logically justify his purchase to keep his WIFE happy.

But it was *emotion* that made him buy.

So, if you wanna make mucho dinero with your email marketing, pack more *emotion* into your emails.

Put your heart and soul into them.

Your emails should have a living and pulsating heart of their own.

Make your subscribers <u>feel</u> something.

Do you sell a weight-loss product?

Make 'em feel what it's like to be skinny.

Do you sell a business opportunity?

Make 'em feel what it's like to be rich.

Do you sell an educational product?

Make 'em feel smart.

Do you sell sports equipment?

Make 'em feel superior.

You feel me?

Verily I say unto you:

If you sell a product or service your subscribers want, and you write promotional emails they like and FEEL, your subscribers will have no choice but to buy!

Hey Kelvin, that was a great little lesson!

Thank you.

Thank you very much.

*"The two most beautiful words in the
English language are 'check enclosed'."*

Dorothy Parker

T he four most beautiful words in the English dictionary for an
email marketer are:

"Notification of payment received."

That's right, for a marketer, when those four words show up in your
inbox, there's no sweeter sight for the eyes.

To see that sweet email eye candy showing up daily in YOUR email
inbox, you're gonna need these two things:

(1) A bunch of subscribers who Know, Like and Trust you.

(2) A product or service they wanna get their hot little hands on.

And when you have these two things, well, it really is a thing of
beauty.

Peace.

John Wayne

I t's an excellent observation, isn't it?

Here's another most excellent observation.

Behold:

There are a helluva lot of marketers out there making email marketing tougher than it need be.

Am I calling these marketers stupid?

Yes.

I am.

Listen, I'm not saying email marketing isn't tough.

It <u>is</u> tough.

And if you're a sensitive little snowflake or you are taking medication for a heart-related issue, then I strongly advise against you pursuing email marketing.

But, assuming you're in good health, there's only one other factor that will determine if email marketing is too tough for your righteous-self.

And that is this:

If you're not the brightest crayon in the pack, email marketing <u>will</u> be extremely tough for you.

But you're one of <u>my</u> subscribers.

And nearly all my subscribers (some slip through the cracks) are highly intelligent individuals, so I don't see this being a problem for you.

That said, I still wanna give you a little list of steps to make *damn* sure your email marketing doesn't get any tougher than it should.

43

Check it out:

(1) Have a good product or service your market <u>wants</u> (screw that part up, nothing will work).

(2) Offer your market something free to "get them in the door," and collect their email address (VERY important part right there).

(3) Send regular emails (one per day is good <u>if</u> you're doing it the "Maverick's way") selling your product or service.

(4) Grow your list of subscribers.

(5) Keep opening and reading The Email Marketing Maverick's emails and implement all that thou readeth.

What did I hear you say?

You say that list is all well and good, but how do you increase sales?

It's a good question, Pookie.

But I have already answered that question on the list I just gave you.

Let me give you a clue:

It ain't step (1), (2), or step (3).

Nope.

It isn't step (4) either!

"A lot of people are afraid of heights. Not me, I'm afraid of widths."

Steven Wright

A lot of email marketers are afraid of unsubscribes. I'm not; I'm afraid of <u>new</u> subscribers.

Listen . . .

. . . being afraid of unsubscribes is like being afraid that the song you're listening to while being put on hold is going to be cut short when your call finally gets put through.

Who the hell cares.

You're not on the phone to listen to Beethoven's Symphony no. 9 In D Minor, you're on the phone to get customer service and have your issue resolved pronto, hopefully by someone whose English you can understand.

Anything other than your issue getting resolved is a waste of your time.

And so it is with email marketing.

What do you care if someone unsubscribes?

They were never gonna buy anyway.

They were wasting their time and your time being on your list.

Trust me. it's better for ALL involved when they unsubscribe.

As for being afraid of new subscribers?

Well, I'm always afraid that "time wasters" are gonna slip through the cracks and crawl onto my list.

But ya know what?

Once these tawdry time wasters get a little taste of the Maverick's ways of doing email, they tend not to hang around very long.

"Everyone probably thinks that I'm a raving nymphomaniac, that I have an insatiable sexual appetite, when the truth is I'd rather read a book."

Madonna

L ove her or hate her, there's no denying Madonna's one helluva marketer and a "maverick" in every sense of the word.

Now, to quote Salt-N-Pepper:

Let's talk about sex.

Sex is one of the most powerful desires and motivations us humans have.

Know this:

A guy who buys a bright red sports car is not just buying a sports car. He's buying something else he secretly (and sometimes subconsciously) wants even more than the sports car itself.

And what is that?

This:

He's buying the "attention" of attractive women he hopes to get when driving his red sports car.

Yep, sex is often the underlying motivating factor of a buyer.

Ignoring this fact in your marketing will make your advertising, well, less sexy.

And easier to ignore.

Why?

Because marketing is all about getting attention, and when it comes to attention-getting, sex is the trump card.

But play that card with caution, my little marketing crony.

Unless you're selling sex toys or something of that nature, I don't need to tell you that sex should be "implied" rather boldly stated, right?

Good.

Just checkin'.

Now, if that above quote from Madonna is true, and I believe it is, then it really does explain a lot of Madonna's success.

You see, she put out what her market wanted, not what she wanted.

Giving your market what you want is dumb.

Give your market what THEY want, not what YOU want.

Your wants are even more irrelevant than the 'b' in the word dumb.

A music video full of books and literature and people reading was not gonna cut through to her market.

Maybe if they were all wearing . . . ah, never mind.

The bottom line?

Utilize the power of sex in your sales message (implied, of course), and care very much about what your market wants, and care very little about what you want.

Do this, and your customers will keep comin' back for more.

"Anybody can play.
The note is only 20 percent.
The attitude of the motherf*cker
who plays it is 80 percent."

Miles Davis

C ouldn't agree more.

You know, I think that quote is even more applicable to email marketing.

Any mo' fo' can write a promotional email, but very few people have the necessary attitude required to write emails that pull in the bucks once the send button's been pushed.

Hey, listen.

They say you should keep a close eye on your competition, you know, to see what they're up to and how they go about doing what they do.

But that would require me to read other marketers promotional emails.

And ya know what?

I'd rather gouge my eyes out with a tablespoon than have to read their vapid emails.

You see, the way most marketers write their promotional emails, in my opinion, makes the marketer come across as flakey as a pastry puff.

These marketers lack the #1 quality in email marketing that determines if you win (increase profits) or lose (not increase profits).

And that my friend, is . . .

. . . Having The Attitude Of A Maverick!

What exactly is a "maverick attitude?"

Good question, Chief.

A maverick attitude means:

(1) You care more about what you are doing than what your competition is doing.

(2) You do things your way for no other reason than that's the way you wanna do it.

(3) You don't pretend to care for your subscribers or customers; you DO genuinely care for your them.

(4) You don't pamper, kiss butt, or put your subscribers on a pedestal. You respect them. They must respect you. If they give any disrespect, you tell 'em not to let the unsubscribe button hit 'em on their way out. That's right. You unsubscribe their sorry ass.

My motto's: "If they've got no class, they're out on their ass!"

(5) You believe in what you're selling.

(6) You don't shy away from selling, in fact, you love it!

(7) You promote your service or product with all the gusto and commitment of a kamikaze pilot.

(8) You state your opinion in no uncertain terms.

(9) You don't take yourself, business, or even life too seriously.

(10) You take serving your subscribers and customers VERY seriously.

(11) You never just "phone in" an email. Every promotional email you send your list has the heart and soul of a Bruce Springsteen performance.

(12) Your #1 focus is making damn sure you deliver the best product or service humanly possible.

That, my friend, is the "maverick attitude."

But alas . . .

. . . this list of requirements automatically disqualifies most people.

Now listen good:

Not knowing how to write emails that bring in the cabbage is not a major problem IF you have the "maverick attitude."

Why?

Cuz I could teach you the "hows" of writing emails that bring in the green in a matter of weeks if you were serious enough.

But, not having the "maverick attitude" IS a major problem.

Here's why:

Because if you don't possess the maverick attitude, it wouldn't matter what I taught you—it simply wouldn't work.

Why?

Because selling is 80% attitude (if not more) and 20% skill.

You could have all the "copywriting chops" in the world, but without the maverick attitude, well, selling your product or service will be harder to sell than a book titled: LANCE ARMSTRONG— A PORTRAIT OF INTEGRITY.

"Honestly, if I had taken this whole career thing seriously, I would've named it something else besides Foo Fighters. It's the worst F*CKING band name in the world."

Dave Grohl

N ames are highly overrated.

You know, there are a ton of companies, bands, or even people with lousy names that are uber successful.

You can't tell me Google, Amazon, eBay, Walmart, and Ikea are good names.

They're as dull as dishwater.

Listen.

Saying that a *name* makes a brand, is like saying that your kid's name is the determining factor on whether they become successful or not.

It simply isn't true.

Look, I'm all for having a great brand name, I mean, I'm called: The Email Marketing Maverick—you can't get much better than that, right?

HEY! No need to be like that.

Geez.

Anyways, in my prideful opinion, your brand name has very little bearing on how successful your company, music band, or person you'll become.

Because it's the people (or person) behind the brand name that will determine its success.

You know, Dave Grohl could've called his band "Racoon Turd," and it wouldn't have made any difference.

Why?

Cuz it's Dave Grohl that made the name "Foo Fighters" great.

Dave Grohl's songs, attitude, and his band members are what people grew to love.

Look, let's say you're the owner of a fitness gym.

You come up with the name: Incredible Bulk, which I think is a very good name.

But, you're an overweight fitness trainer that smokes, has only second-hand equipment that's half-rusted, and you have the business acumen of Lindsay Lohan.

Sure, that cool business name (Incredible Bulk) might draw some attention, and pull in a few new customers for a while, UNTIL they realize how incredibly substandard and pathetic your gym is.

Now that cool name (Incredible Bulk) isn't so "cool." Incredible Bulk is now only associated with negativity.

That's right, YOU through being completely inept in every way, turned a potentially good name, into a bad name.

And so it is with YOUR name in regards to email marketing.

I'll explain:

You see, marketers get all excited about subject lines.

They're always dreaming up clever subject lines to boost their open rates.

But then they send their subscribers substandard and pathetic emails that give zero value.

Well, that's like coming up with a clever business name to attract new customers but then delivering a shoddy product or service.

It won't last.

People might get tricked once or twice, but then they'll simply stop turning up, or for us email marketers, stop opening up our emails.

Hear me on this:

If you wanna increase your email open rate, focus less on coming up with clever subject lines and focus more on delivering value-packed emails your subscribers will love.

If you do that, it won't be long before your subscribers start opening your emails just because YOU sent them.

It's YOU and the quality of your emails that will ultimately determine if your open rates will be good in the long run, not your clever subject lines.

You know, I want every single one of my emails to be so damn good, so easy to read, so entertaining, so relevant, so helpful that when my subscribers see my name: Kelvin Dorsey show up in their inbox, they open.

Listen:

When you're consistently sending emails that your subscribers love to read, then your subject lines become less and less of a factor on whether your subscribers open the email or not.

Just seeing the sender's name (your name) in their inbox with be enough.

So, if you have no shame to your email game, there'll be no shame to your name, only fame!

Boy that sounded hokey, didn't it?

At least I tried, right?

Ah whadda you care.

I'm done helping you today.

Aristotle

H ave you ever been walking alongside a friend, then all of a sudden, your friend clumsily trips over?

Have you seen someone walk head-first into a glass door?

I know you have.

And, I also <u>know</u> how you reacted to seeing such a thing.

You would've had one of following three responses:

(1) A wry smile broke out on your face.

(2) You sniggered to yourself.

(3) You had a good ol' belly laugh.

How do I know?

Human nature, my friend.

We're all the same.

Even the most uptight folks with vapid personalities and no sense of humor will laugh at someone who slips on a banana peel and lands flat on their ass.

We can't help it.

It's the "element of surprise" Aristotle identified that triggers a little chuckle in us all.

Aristotle claims that surprise is the secret to humor, and I believe he's spot on with that.

Isn't that reassuring, that good ol' Kelvin, The Email Marketing Maverick gives the thumbs up to Aristotle's claims?

Whatever.

Look, I have a little secret myself.

Wanna know what my little secret is?

It's a secret that will fill your coffers to overflowing.

Well, do ya?

Ok, it's this: Get people to like you.

You see, people do business with people they like.

So, the secret to making more bucks with your email marketing is . . .

. . . Get Your Subscribers To LIKE You!

So simple, yet so ignored by many marketers.

Understand this:

One of the most powerful and effective ways to get your subscribers to like you is to use humor.

Listen . . .

EVERYONE loves to hang with the guy or gal who can make them laugh, but NOBODY wants to hang around a bore.

So, for crying out loud, stop being a bore in your emails.

Write emails that have some humor.

Okay, Kelvin, I wanna get my subscribers to like me more, but how do I inject humor into my emails?

I thought you'd ask that.

It's pretty simple.

Stop being so predictable.

Predictability goes against the very nature of humor.

Surprise your subscribers with subject lines they are not used to seeing.

Tell stories that haven't heard before.

Say things they wouldn't expect you to say.

Vary up your emails.

Keep them guessing.

You wanna keep your subscribers on their toes like a midget at a urinal.

Surprise them, surprise them, surprise them!

Alright . . .

I'm gonna finish with a joke from standup comedian Sarah Silverman that uses the "element of surprise" that, well, makes it funny.

Here it is:

"My sister was with two men in one night.
She could hardly walk after that.
Can you imagine?
Two dinners!"

"I really like a lot of kinds of music, but the blues just does something to my insides."

Johnny Winter

I feel the same way about marketing, Johnny Winter! (God rest his soul.)

I really like a lot of the marketing mediums out there today.

Facebook ads, YouTube ads, Twitter, pay per click—they're all great.

But what really warms the cockles of my heart is good ol' email.

Ah yes, Email.

She's not the spritely young mistress she used to be.

Years of harsh and abusive treatment from marketers have taken its toll on this once young and vigorous marketing medium.

The signs of aging are there for all to see—sagging email open rates and less than perky opt-in rates.

This is email's current reality.

But savvy marketers the world over still love her.

Why?

Because she keeps on "putting out" for her marketers more than any other marketing medium.

Boy, I'm really milking this analogy, aren't I?

Yes, as far as making sales goes, email is still the one.

None can compete with her ROI.

And in the marketing game, that's everything.

Do your own research on email marketing and compare her to other marketing mediums, and see for yourself.

You'll see that . . .

. . . Email Is The Great Matriarch Of The Marketing Mediums!

And . . .

. . . I love her.

*"Conquering the world on horseback
is easy; it is dismounting and
governing that is hard."*

Genghis Khan

G etting subscribers is easy, it's getting sales that is hard.

You know, I had a good hard think about why this is the case.

And here's what my brilliant mind came up with after much contemplation:

"Why the hell are you asking me?! I have no idea!"

But, I am a hard taskmaster.

So I reprimanded my mind and put it straight back to work. Lo and behold, it came up with an answer I think maybe THE answer.

Would you like to hear it?

Okay.

Here's why I think the act of *making sweet sales* is indeed harder than the act of *getting subscribers.*

Because getting a subscriber is simply a matter of getting their attention and interest, whereas getting a subscriber to buy, involves having credibility and proof.

First, let's look at the process of getting subscribers.

Yep, getting subscribers is not that hard a dance to do.

Cuz let's face it, any schmuck can get someone's attention.

I mean, the drunk at the bar who just farted will get attention, n'est pas?

I tell ya, *attention-getting* really is the at the bottom of the sales and marketing food chain.

A slightly harder, but still a monkey-simple skill, is getting someone's *interest*.

Now back to the drunk at the bar. Yup, even the local drunk could get someone's interest by offering to buy someone a drink.

I for one, would not discriminate on such an offer. If you're a buyin', I'm a drinkin'.

So, as you can see, getting subscribers is as easy as farting at a bar and offering to buy a patron a beer.

Now, getting a subscriber to pony up and <u>buy</u> is a whole other matter.

You see, getting your subscribers to buy requires you to <u>prove</u> that what you promise to deliver, your product or service will, in fact, DO what you say it will DO.

Yeah, I know, it really sucks how demanding subscribers are these days.

It really would be easier if they just took us at our word, right?

But alas . . .

. . . the reality is that subscribers today are . . .

. . . More Skeptical Than an Atheist In Church!

But fear ye not, there IS an easy way to overcome your subscriber's deep-seated skepticism.

Not only will this easy way smack the living skepticism outta them, but it will also make you appear as trustworthy as a close friend and as credible as a Nobel Prize winner.

Sounds too good to be true?

It ain't.

Here's the secret:

The secret's in the follow-up.

But not just any old email follow-up.

NO!

Doing email follow-up the way other marketers do it will leave you with skinny kids.

I'm talking about email follow-up the Maverick's way.

What you do is, you send them charming emails where you let your personality shine through like a diamond on a dead man's finger. Sorry, bad simile.

I mean like the morning sunlight through your bedroom window.

Better?

Now, to think that advice is too hokey, or a little contrived is a mistake.

A BIG mistake.

This is where almost every biz owner falls down with their email marketing. They write emails that are about as personal as a Christmas card from a bank.

And as a result, their subscribers never grow to know, like, or trust them.

You must humanize your email communications for bonding to take place.

Now, if thou wilt harken unto me, and do it the Maverick's way, and really let your personality shine through, over time, your subscribers will start to see you as a true friend, and not just some slimy marketer who's trying to crawl into their wallets.

But folk aren't going to buy just cuz they like you.

No sir.

I don't care how likable you are; if your subscribers aren't fully convinced that YOU, your product, or service will deliver on your promise, you will not see a single penny.

So, to avoid this all too common scenario, do as follows:

Simply prove to them that you ARE someone credible, someone who is an authority in your field, someone, who does have a quality product or service.

You do this by actually helping them.

I know this is a novel concept to most marketers, but you know what?

Nowadays, even your marketing has to help your prospect in some way.

Now, I'm not suggesting you give the farm away on this concept of helping your prospect.

I mean, if they want real help, they gotta pony-up and buy your product or service, right?

Damn straight.

But you should be getting them a small win or a result that takes them closer to their desired goal.

And sending regular emails full of helpful and insightful information that your subscribers want (key word right there) will not only help them to get a small win, but it will prove to your subscribers that you are the most credible guy or gal to buy from.

Once you've done all this, you will have risen high above the hoi polloi, and when your subscribers are ready to buy . . .

. . . it will be your loving arms they run to with credit card in hand.

How sweet it is.

For Serious Marketers ONLY

A s the title plainly says, this section is for serious marketers only.

I'm referring to marketers who:

!. Have a product or service

2. Have a list of subscribers

3. Want to dramatically boost their email open rates click throughs, and sales

If that's you, you may want to check out a free digital product I created.

It's called: The Ultimate Cheat-Sheet (17 Email Types your subscribers will love to read and buy from)

This free digital product will show you how to apply the wisdom and principles in this book to email marketing.

If you're interested, you can grab it here: Ultimate Email Cheat-Sheet

"I fear it as little as to drink a cup of tea."

Ned Kelly

That was Ned Kelly's response when asked, "Are you afraid to die?" right before he was going to be hanged.

As you can see, it wasn't just Ned Kelly's head protection that was made of steel.

Now, on the topic of being afraid, hear this: Many a marketer has failed miserably at email marketing because of fear.

A common fear that keeps them writing lame, vapid emails is this:

The fear of offending their subscribers.

I don't fear offending subscribers; I LOVE it.

It's sport to me.

It's what makes email marketing fun.

Listen, you should <u>purposefully</u> offend subscribers.

Hmm, I'm sensing bad vibes from you right now, maybe I should explain myself.

I wouldn't want to offend you now, would I?

But Kelvin, you just finished saying . . .

. . . HEY!

I know it seems like I'm making as much sense as a circular firing squad, but that's because as much as I love offending subscribers, I also love confusing them.

But don't worry, I won't leave you confused, it's merely an attention keeping tactic I like to employ.

Listen:

When I say offend subscribers, I'm not talking about offending YOU or any other good-hearted and intelligent subscriber of mine.

No sir.

I'm talking about offending the few loser subscribers who somehow find their sorry way onto my list.

You know the ones? The tire kickers, lookie-loo's, freebie hunters, the do-nothings, and the people who are so uptight that if you stuck a lump of coal up their bum, after one week, you'd have a diamond.

Anyway, are you picking up what I'm putting down?

Trust me; you don't want these losers on your list.

They'll put pain in your brain.

You must offend them.

Then offend them again.

Then offend them some more.

Offend Them And Their Evil Ways Right Off Your Righteous List!

And remember, offending these muppets isn't scary, it's fun.

It's almost as fun as making sales.

I said almost.

Try it, you'll see.

*"Good comedy helps people know they're not
alone. Great comedy provides an answer."*

Bill Hicks

Y ou wanna start your emails *good* and then end 'em *great*.
Yeah, yeah . . . I'll explain.

By starting off *good*, I mean this:

You want to get in sync with your subscribers.

Let them know you understand them.

Ever spoken to someone who's going through a similar problem as you?

I bet you have, and I bet you were all ears, too. People love to listen to others who "get them" or understand what they're going through.

It makes them feel like they're not alone.

And this is good.

But it's not great.

Here's how you finish off your emails *great*.

Understand this:

Your subscribers have subscribed to you because they're interested in your service or product.

Let me be even clearer.

They have a problem that your product or service can solve.

Your subscribers are looking for answers.

So . . .

. . . Provide them!

Tell me, does your product or service provide an answer?

Then why on earth are you not letting your subscribers know about it?

If your product or service provides your prospects with a solution to their problem, you're doing them no favors holding it back.

You know, most biz owners are so timid and shy about promoting their products, their emails sound more like an apology than a sales pitch.

Look, if you wanna fatten your business profits with email, then you gotta promote your wares like Kim Kardashian promotes her patootie—shamelessly, audaciously and all the time.

Any promotional email that ends with a big-ass sales pitch is a <u>great</u> email.

So there you go . . . I've just given you the template to the perfect promotional email—from good to great.

Yep, thems the rules.

"Talent without working hard is nothing."

Cristiano Ronaldo

T oday . . .

. . . I'm going to give you, what I believe, is the greatest secret to success you could ever learn.

This secret to success pertains to any field of endeavor, activity, or venture you may undertake, not just email marketing.

It's an ancient secret to success that throughout history has taken ordinary men and women and propelled them to places of leadership, influence and great eminence.

Are you getting excited yet?

Don't get too excited, Buckwheat.

You ain't gonna like this secret very much.

Nobody does.

I guess that's why there are so few highly successful people in the world.

Anyway, I've strung you along enough here, let me reveal the greatest secret to success to you by quoting a popular saying.

"The harder I work, the luckier I get."

Yes, all things being equal, when it comes to achieving success, *hard work* is . . .

. . . The Greatest Secret Of Them All!

Huh! I told you that you wouldn't like it.

What did you say?

You think I'm overvaluing the importance of hard work?

You think that intelligence, talent, upbringing, and your current network have more of an influence on your success than plain old working hard?

Well, let me answer that by quoting a man who understood success and achievement possibly better than almost any other man— Alexander Graham Bell:

"A man owes very little to what he is born with.
A man is what he makes of himself."

Hear, hear!

And here's another thing: Don't buy into the "work smarter not harder" philosophy.

This ear tickling phrase is the lazy man's mantra.

Let me tell you something.

Yes, there <u>are</u> smarter ways to do things.

There <u>are</u> certain insights you can pick up along the way that can shortcut your journey to success.

And would you like to know <u>who</u> the people are that discover these shortcuts and smarter ways to do things?

Okay, I'll tell you.

The people who discover the "smart way" to do things are . . .

. . . The People Who Work The Hardest!

Now, back to this quote (I don't know who first said "The harder I work the luckier I get" but it really doesn't matter, does it?)

What does matters is this:

That you put the greatest secret to success (hard work) to work in your life, and yes, in your email marketing.

Hey, you know what I'm sick of hearing?

It's this:

"Kelvin, I'm already working 12 hours a day on my business, I don't have the time to write emails every day!"

69

Aww, paw Pookie iz too bwizy to wite sum emails.

Listen . . .

These folks are essentially saying that they don't have time to increase their business profits?

Look, the folks who complain about being too busy to write emails to promote their product, service or business are in fact, just a lost cause.

They simply don't understand the power and ability of email marketing to explode your business profits when done right (The Maverick's way).

And frankly, I'm not the slightest bit interested in trying to convince or educate these ignoramus biz owners on the power of email marketing.

I'd have more luck convincing a card holding, anti-corporation vegan to chow down two Big Macs!

BTW, I just gave you an extremely valuable sales and marketing lesson right there—don't sell to folks who need to be educated on what you have to sell. ONLY sell to folks who understand your product or service and WANT it.

Now, back to the topic of hard work.

I was watching a documentary on Cristiano Ronaldo the other day (It's on YouTube. Hey, what can I say? It's free, and I'm cheap!)

It's called: The Making Of Ronaldo.

What struck me the most, watching this documentary, was a comment made by Ronaldo's high school coach, Paul Clement.

Here's what Paul Clement said:

> *"Ronaldo was no more talented than the rest of the boys. What separated Ronaldo from the rest was how hard this kid worked. That's what gave him the edge."*

And guess what?

Anybody who's successfully increased their businesses profits with email marketing didn't do it by sheer chance, or by natural talent, or by copying their competition.

No, no, no.

Their email marketing was successful because they worked harder on their email game than their lazy competitors.

That's right, they rolled up their sleeves, got down on their knees, and sunk their fingernails deep into the email marketing dirt and . . .

. . . Dug Like Crazy Until They Struck Email Marketing Gold!

In case I'm being a little too metaphor-happy for you, when I say "email marketing gold," I mean: Increase of Business Profits.

Yep, more bucks, bones, chedda, green stuff, whatever you wanna call it.

I mean, isn't that the whole goal of email marketing and business— to make sales and increase profits?

Make no mistake; the goal is <u>always</u> sales.

Sales are how we keep score in the game of email marketing.

Email marketing without sales is like playing an entire soccer match (I know they call it football—I don't!) without scoring a single goal.

That's called:

Losing!

Personally, I'm more into winning.

Now listen . . .

. . . If you wanna kick more goals (make more sales) with your email marketing, you simply need to work harder on your email game than your competitors work on theirs.

And guess what?

That's an incredibly easy thing to do.

Why?

Cuz hardly anybody is working on their email game.

They may do email marketing, but they sure as hell aren't working on improving it.

They prefer to blindly put all their faith into tools like; autoresponders; subject line checkers; visual website optimizers, and the other kind of 'Tools', so-called 'email marketing experts' who analyze (notice the first 4 letters of that word) and track every statistic other than the one stat that really matters—SALES!

Okay, Kelvin, I hear what you're saying, but how do I work on my email marketing game?

You know, I really like how you ask me just the right question at just the right time.

And here's my answer to you:

You should do the following 4 things:

The first thing you should do upon getting out of bed (preferably before 5:00 am) is to chug down 750 ml of water and then break out into 70 crunches followed by 350 sit ups and then cap it off with a hand-stand in which you hold for 15 minutes.

This should get your body all limbered up and make your mind super alert, ready to start writing your first promotional email for the day.

Wow Kelvin!, do you really do all that every morning?

Nope.

I hate exercise.

But, you asked me what you <u>should</u> do, and I think that early morning routine would probably be a very positive thing for you to do.

But if you hate getting up early and exercising as much as me, then simply skip the first step.

Let's move to step #2

Practice your copywriting skills.

Yes, I'm talking about approaching "copywriting" like you would a soccer training session.

What do they do at soccer training, or any other sport, for that matter?

That's right. They do *drills* to get their skills razor sharp.

But you can't do drills with copywriting, right?

WRONG!

There's plenty of drills you can perform when it comes to copywriting.

Now, imagine this scenario.

Let's say that you ask me—The Maverick—to be your copywriting coach.

I inform you on how much money you would need to pay me.

And after picking yourself up off the ground upon hearing my exorbitant fee—and paying me that exorbitant fee—I would set the following drills for you to relentlessly go over and over and over.

Here are those drills:

Go to a reputable copywriting blog that has swipe files (a collection of winning sales letters) and copy those sales letters out by hand.

Huh?

You wanna know how many sales letters you should copy in your own handwriting and how often?

Ahh, you were doing so well until you asked that lame-brain question.

Look . . .

. . . It depends on how good you wanna be.

If you really want to amp up your email game and write such persuasive sales copy that your readers start frantically reaching for their credit cards while reading your copy, then . . .

. . . you'll copy out as many sales letters as you can, and you'll do it as often as you can!

Pure and simple.

Onward.

Next, I'd get you to do the exact same exercise, but this time, you'll be copying out a collection of bullets.

Then you do the same with headlines.

BTW, a great website for these drills is called: Hard To Find Ads.

It has a great collection of winning sales letters, bullets, and headlines written from the world's best copywriters.

Next, I would get you reading some good fiction books.

Why?

To get your storytelling chops up.

A crucial skill to hone the email marketing game.

Next, I would get you to do market research.

You can never do this too much.

The more you know about your market, the better.

If you don't have a deep understanding of your market, you're screwed.

Most folks who are struggling online are as confused as a senior citizen with an iPod when it comes to knowing their market.

They don't have a specific group of people identified as their target market.

And even if they have a specific group of people, they're clueless about what these folk really hate and really love.

Now, let's get a little more practical with our market research.

Here's what I would get you to do:

Go to Amazon.com and look at all the books that are selling well in your industry, niche or market, and read through all the reviews (3 to 4-star reviews are best. A lot of the 5-star reviews these days are as fake as a 3 dollar bill).

This will give your righteous-self a ton of insight into your market's likes and dislikes.

Next, I'd get you to find some of the top online forums in your market.

What you want to do in these forums is just be a fly on a wall.

What are the hot topics and discussions going on in there?

You'll learn a lot about your market. People really speak their minds in these forums.

They're basically telling you all their hot-buttons and thus how to "sell" to them.

It's gold for us marketers.

So there you go . . .

. . . I've just given you an "email marketing game workout" that will give you that Ronaldo Edge over your competition.

The only questions that remains . . .

Do you have that "Ronaldo work ethic" to do it?

"I am indebted to my father for living,
but to my teacher for living well."

Alexander The Great

N ow, I dunno who got you into this game of email marketing, but let me tell you this:

I'm hell-bent on being the teacher YOU credit for doing it well.

By "well" I mean: Making mucho dinero with your promotional emails.

Hey, listen.

Did you know that one of Alexander the Great's most influential teachers was Aristotle?

Yes, it's true.

Alexander the Great took what he'd learned at the feet of Aristotle and went on to conquer the world (literally).

Listen, my little marketing crony, if you wanna go out and conquer the marketplace and take your share, then you must master email marketing.

Email marketing is the most efficient and powerful weapon you have at your disposal.

How <u>well</u> you wield this weapon of mass influence and persuasion will determine how much market share you take.

Let me ask you this:

If Aristotle was alive today, what do you think his advice would be to email marketers who are trying to persuade their subscribers to buy their product or service?

Well, we don't need to guess my friend, because I can tell you exactly what Aristotle would say.

He would say exactly what he said to folks 2,400 years ago when they asked him how they could become more persuasive.

And that is this:

To use the three points of persuasion:

Ethos (credibility)

Pathos (emotion)

Logos (intellect/logic)

You see, human nature never changes, therefore, neither do the elements that cause people to be persuaded and influenced.

And the way humans are influenced and persuaded are by the three elements Aristotle called, "The 3 points of persuasion."

BTW, don't think you can persuade someone with just 1 or 2 of the 3 points of persuasion.

That's like trying to sit on a three-legged stool that has a missing leg.

So, make sure you're packin' all 3 persuasion points in all your emails and, well, you'll start taking market share like Alexander The Great took pieces of land.

Okay, class dismissed.

You know, when it comes to email marketing, I think I may just be the modern-day Aristotle.

Maybe I should change my name to The Aristotle Of Email Marketing, eh?

Nah, it's much more fun being the Maverick.

I can get away with more that way.

"When you're not practicing,
someone else is getting better."

Allen Iverson

When you're not sending emails to your list, someone else IS. And they're getting YOUR business.

Yep, short and sour today.

*"The only thing that interferes with
my learning is my education."*

Albert Einstein

A nd so it is with email marketing.

You see, people who come into email marketing with a high degree of English writing skills (PhDs in literature being the worst) are never the best email marketers.

An email <u>is</u> really just a sales pitch for your product or service.

An email is NOT a piece of literature.

You're writing for sales, not applause.

Never forget that.

"I am the literary equivalent of a Big Mac and fries."

Stephen King

Y up, Mr. King is the first to admit he's not the greatest of writers.

But I suspect that doesn't worry him too much when he checks his bank account or his book sales.

You see, the heart and soul of fiction writing is storytelling.

And when it comes to storytelling, King is king.

What's all this got to do with *you* writing emails that bring in the green?

Lots.

Listen, you may not be a great writer either (technically speaking).

But worry not, my literary challenged friend, because great writing is not what it takes to make moolah with email marketing.

So what does it take?

Salesmanship, my friend, salesmanship.

Why is this?

Hey, keep the questions comin', this is good.

Well, because the heart and soul of email marketing are sales (selling).

Get good at *that*; you've got this email marketing thing licked.

"There is but one path.
We must kill them all."

Spartacus (Starz TV Show)

I think you'd have to agree, to achieve anything in life it takes the following four qualities:

(1) Motivation (2) Focus (3) Action (4) Persistence.

Uh huh, I knew you'd agree.

Now, imagine this: You have four crazed criminals charging at you, all armed with swords and spiked balls on chains, with one intent in mind—to turn you into minced meat! And if *they* don't succeed, there will be an ambush of starved and bloodthirsty tigers released to finish you off.

Scary thought, ain't it?

Well, that's exactly what the ancient gladiators had to deal with in the Roman coliseums.

Now let me ask you a silly question: Do you think the Gladiators struggled to find "motivation" in this situation?

Of course not. It's kill or be killed, right?

Ok, here's another silly question: Do you think these gladiators struggled to focus or take action or persist in that situation?

Again, of course not.

Now listen to this:

Most folks are not achieving their desired goals in life because they do not understand how the human psyche works.

Let me explain: Have you ever tried to achieve a goal and completely failed? (Are you getting tired of my silly questions yet?)

Maybe you tried to go on a diet, or increase your income, or buy all my products and start implementing all my teachings, or whatever.

But alas, you just couldn't persist, right? So what did you do? I bet you either just gave up, or if you have a little bit of fight in you, you probably grit your teeth and tried again, but to no avail.

What's going on here?

Why can't people persist until they reach their goals? (Now that's a *good* question, eh?)

Well, I'll tell you, and trust me, I know whereof I speak. I have failed to persist on my personal goals more times than Thomas Edison failed while trying to invent the light globe.

Now here's the answer:

People fail to persist on their goals because they simply aren't motivated enough.

That's right, they just sorta kinda wanting their goal, and that, will never be enough.

Listen: All great accomplishment comes from a burning desire from within. Now, to keep things simple, let's use the word: 'motivation' to describe this burning desire, okay?

Now, remember how I said there are four qualities needed to achieve something in life?

Well, the truth is, you need only to focus on but one of the four qualities to achieve your goals.

You see, if you, like those gladiators, are truly motivated, then guess what?

Well, you won't have to worry about being focused, or taking action, or being persistent. Why?

It's simple: Because those three qualities are all driven by your motivation.

Nah, you're still not getting it. Let me see if I can't make it a little clearer for you.

Listen: If your motivation is weak, so will your focus be. And if your focus is weak, so will your actions be. And if your actions are weak, you will not persist.

Okay, Kelvin, you're putting forth a convincing case, but can you increase your motivation, and if so, how?

Ahh, that's what I like about you, Buckwheat, you ask just the right questions, at just the right time.

Alright, here is my answer:

Yes, I believe you can.

Look, if you run your own business, you already have, by default, more reasons to be motivated than the average person.

The average person (employee) suckles at the tit of employment, whether motivated or not. The employee does just enough work not to get fired, and the employer pays them just enough to keep them. Yep, a motivated employee is about as rare as unicorn meat.

But for us biz owners, we only get paid if we run a successful business.

But you know what?

Sometimes not even having your own business can be enough to motivate you to the point of persisting with your business or life goals.

You see, motivation can disappear quicker than Tyra Bank's music career if you're not careful.

So what's the secret to staying highly motivated?

Would you like the quick answer?

Too bad. I really wanna make damn sure you get this, and for you to get it, I'm going to need to set it up first.

Here's the setup: Being in business for yourself is just like being a Roman gladiator fighting in the Colosseum.

Here's how: You may not have crazed criminals and wild animals trying to kill you, but that doesn't mean you don't have any opposition that must be fought off.

In fact, you have many things opposing you that if you don't get motivated, focused, take action, and persist you will be overcome and defeated by these forces.

What are these opposing forces?

Hmm, about these:

Your Competition.

Yep, if you don't get motivated, then your target market will simply find a business owner that is.

Time

Let's face it. You're not the young stallion you used to be. And if you're not motivated, time becomes your enemy instead of your ally. You see, in five years' time, you're either going to be glad or sad. It all depends on what you've been doing over those five years.

Impact

Ahh, now this one's a biggie. Most folks are walking around in life as miserable as Andy Murray after losing at Wimbledon (or just Andy Murray in general, actually).

Why is this? I'm glad you asked. Well, would you allow Dr. Kelvin to elucidate?

Why thank you.

Now hear this: Most folks don't get this, but what really makes us humans happy, is not doing things for ourselves, but rather doing things to help others.

It's the most damn counterintuitive thing you'll ever learn. But it's true nonetheless.

Now think about this: You being a business owner have a huge opportunity to become very happy? How so?

Here's how so: Well, think about it, doesn't your product or service help people in some way? Well, that is what you should be focusing on. Not only will it help improve your product and service but it will make you happier knowing you're touching lives in a positive way.

That's right, you're improving people's lives, and that is the real source of happiness my friend.

You see, most folks have lost sight of the fact that business is really service to mankind. It's a way to improve people's way of life. I know it's easy to forget this if you've ever found yourself in the financial ketchup and the wolves are at the door.

At times like that, it's very easy to be you-focused. I mean screw helping people, I just need some money to keep my lights on, right? I hear ya, but know this:

Helping others with your service or product is what brings in the bucks, so really, you are forced to focus on others.

But if you truly do focus on improving the lives of others and want to impact people for good, not only will you start making more green, but you'll find your bad-self becoming happier.

You know, I didn't mean to go on and on about this, but I suspect I needed to hear this just as much as you (probably a whole lot more).

Anyway, I hope this has helped you as much as it's helped me writing it. See, there I go again, I'm trying first to help myself. I told you this "focus on helping others" thing is not easy.

Okay, let sum this up:

If you want to increase your motivation to the point where you take persistent action until you arrive at all your goals, then focus on the three aforementioned points; your competition, your time, and your impact.

Do all this, and you'll be more motivated than, umm, I dunno, a really motivated person.

Hey, I can't always come up with a clever simile, you know.

Oh wait, what about this: You'll be more motivated than Tony Robbins finding out he only has three months to live.

Does that work?

Alright, until next time, keep on keepin' on.

"My greatest teacher was not a vocal coach, not the work of other singers, but the way Tommy Dorsey breathed and phrased on the trombone."

Frank Sinatra

L et me say this:

My greatest marketing teachers are not the great direct marketers and copywriters of the world, but the way comedians connect with an audience and sell their point of views with great humor.

"Truth is, I'm a fucking romantic. I'm difficult but I promise I'm not boring."

Amy Winehouse

Y ou know, in regard to email marketing, if you just don't be boring, you'll be light years ahead of all the other marketers out there.

You know I'm right.

*"Do I have to know rules and all
that crap? Then forget it."*

John Daly

That was John Daly's reply when asked if he would join the Royal And Ancient Golf Club, after winning the 1995 Open at St. Andrews.

Huh, love it.

My exact sentiments.

You know, golf has a ton of pompous corporate stiffs who like to parade around the country clubs.

They are more concerned about club membership, clubhouse rules, golf etiquette, and golf rules than they are the actual playing of golf.

John Daly cares for none of that. Daly just loves the playing of golf.

And guess what?

Email marketing has its fair share of corporate stiffs too. They're more interested in best practices, analytics, design, and other industry standards than they are the real business of email marketing, which is, writing damn persuasive emails that bring in the bucks.

Forget all that other crap. Just learn to write persuasive emails that convert into sales.

Trust me. It's a whole lot more profitable (and fun).

"Wise men speak because they have something to say;
fools because they have to say something."

Plato

Y ou know, most email marketers have nothing to say, and they keep on saying it until they lose all readership.

Listen, if you want readership, you'd better have something worth reading.

You should be writing emails to your list because you have something to say, not because you feel you have to say something.

Words to do email by, my friend.

"Rollin' down the street, smokin'
indo, sippin' on gin an juice."

Snoop Dogg

Now that's exactly how I want my subscribers to feel after reading my emails.

Unrealistic?

I dunno?

Too lofty an idea?

Maybe.

But damn it, you've gotta aim for something, haven't you? Why not aim high? (No pun intended.)

Write emails that make people *feel* good.

Do you wanna know how I feel after reading other marketer's emails?

Well, if I had to write a little rap for it, it would go something like this:

"Shufflin' down the road when it's cold and rainy; got holes in ya shoes and ya thoughts are hazy."

"To be with the others, you have to have your hair short and wear ties. So we're trying to make a third world happen, you know what I mean?"

Jimi Hendrix

I'm not a team player.

I hate authority.

And the very thought of working for someone else makes my bum hairs prickle.

Yep, the concept of working to grow someone *else's* business and not your *own*, makes about as much sense as a circular firing squad, to me.

And that is why I love email marketing.

It's the ultimate one-man business.

If I had to explain email marketing in one word, it would be this:

FREEDOM!

"[You] gotta find that inner strength and just pull that sh#t out of you. And get that motivation to not give up. And not be a quitter, no matter how bad you wanna just fall on your face and collapse."

Eminem

P eople sometimes ask me, "How do you come up with all that content and ideas for emails, and how do you find the time, and do it so consistently?"

My answer?

I'll defer to Eminem on that question (read the above quote again).

*"The major incentive to productivity
and efficiency are social and moral
rather than financial."*

Peter Drucker

H ear this, my little marketing crony:

If you want your subscribers to buy your product or service, you can't just natter on about money.

I don't care if you're selling a "make money online" product, you still shouldn't be going on and on about the "bones."

Yes, money's a great carrot. However, it ain't the whole carrot (it's probably just the tip of the carrot).

The major part of the carrots (incentives) are *other* motivating forces that make money pale in comparison.

You see, (most) folk *aren't* obsessed with moolah as much as you think they are.

That said, it doesn't mean they aren't obsessing.

Ohh, they're obsessing alright.

They're obsessing over:

Feeling special, important, and significant.

Sex.

Social status.

Appearance.

Freedom from fear, stress, and pain.

The lust for power.

Care and protection of loved ones.

Those, my friend, are what your subscribers are obsessing over.

And, they are the things that really drive and motivate us humans.

How do I know this is the case?

That's easy.

Cuz *I* obsess over those things. And if you're honest with yourself, so do you.

Yes, indeedy, we're all insecure. Even the most seemingly bold and confident of folks are riddled with insecurities.

Anyway, the point is, make sure you're focusing on what your subscribers are *really* obsessing over.

So, if you really want to turn a buyer on—more talky-talky about those (aforementioned) things and less talky-talky about money.

Simply look at how your product or service helps fulfill those obsessions and, well, you're off to the races.

Actually, more like bank.

*"I don't deal in technique,
I deal in emotions."*

Jimmy Page

M usicians and email marketers are in the same game. The game of emotions.

The musician tries to get his listener to *shake* their booty, and the marketer tries to get his prospect to hand over their booty.

Both require emotion.

If a listener isn't feelin it, they ain't dancin'.

If a prospect isn't feelin' it, they ain't buyin'.

It's that simple.

Listen up: If you truly desire more sales, you'd better start selling to your subscriber's emotions.

Make them feel the pain, suffering, and hell of not getting their problem solved, and, make them feel the euphoria, utopia, and joyful bliss of their problem finally solved by your product or service.

You feel me?

Good.

Class dismissed.

"I miss my brother.
Prince was a funny cat.
Great sense of humor."

Spike Lee

D o you drink coffee?
  I do.

Three a day in fact.

I have one first thing upon waking—always with a biscuit or some type of chocolate.

I never used to have chocolate or biscuits with my coffee.

No, not because I used to be more health conscious or anything, but because I used to have a piece of English cake called Madeira cake with every drink of coffee.

This particular Madeira cake was truly sent from the patisserie gods.

I kid you not; I had that Madeira cake with my coffee for about three straight years.

But then something tragic happened.

No, I didn't develop diabetes or anything like that. No, what happened is, the cake company (One Tops) suddenly stopped making it.

Can you believe that?

Well, I was devastated.

So it came to pass that I set out to find me some other brands of Madeira cake to fill the void One Tops so cruelly left in my sweet, sugar-deprived heart.

And, I *did* find some other brands of Madeira cake, but alas, none compared to my first love (One Tops).

All these other brands of Madeira cake were far inferior and left me more unsatisfied than Michael Douglas at, well . . . any place where there are no women.

Hey, does it seem weird to you that I miss this cake this much?

Yeah, I guess it is a little.

But damn it, you should've tasted that cake.

And, I bet you're wondering where the email marketing lesson is in all this talk of coffee and cake, right?

Well, you can stop wondering cuz I'm about to tell you.

Here starteth thee lesson:

Let me start with a question.

If you suddenly stopped sending emails to your list of subscribers, would they miss hearing from you?

It's a good question to ask, don't you think?

You know, my goal is to write promotional emails that my subscribers love to read—so much so that if I ever stopped sending them, my subscribers would be left devastated and wanting more.

I want *my* subscribers to miss my emails like Tiger Woods misses his little black book.

I would want to be inundated with emails from my pining subscribers begging me to keep sending them their daily dose of the Maverick's profit-making emails.

A lofty goal?

Yes.

Idealism?

Maybe.

But why not aim for that, eh?

You see, if your subscribers don't look forward to receiving your emails, well, you might as well be promoting your product or service on Myspace.

Hey, are you getting the importance of sending great emails to your subscribers yet?

Aw nuts.

You're not gettin' it, are you?

Let me spell it out for you:

If you send emails your subscribers like to read, they'll like YOU.

If they like you, they'll keep reading your emails and start getting to KNOW you.

And once your subscribers start feeling like they know you, they'll start to TRUST you.

And the golden rule for salesmanship is . . .

. . . Get Them To Like, Know, and Trust You.

If you don't get the lesson I'm trying to get across to you here, I give up, and . . . so should you.

"I don't have a fear of flying;
I have a fear of crashing."

Billy Bob Thornton

Y ou know, when folks say they hate *selling*, what they're really saying is . . .

. . . they hate trying to *convince* people who have about as much interest in their product as Kim Kardashian has in wearing modest clothes.

Look, if you *only* sell to folks who *want* what you're offering, selling will become a whole lot less painful, won't it?

Of course.

But we don't want to settle for just less painful. We want it to be fun, right?

Damn straight.

Well, how do we make email marketing more fun?

There are many ways, Bubba, but I have found there is one way that makes email marketing oh so fun.

And that way is to . . .

. . . Make Sales!

Verily I say, when you know how to write emails that drags in the bucks, you'll be having more fun than Michael Phelps at a house party hosted by Snoop Dog.

Huh?

You say that's an obvious observation?

You say that doesn't really help you in any way?

Oh, you want the nitty-gritty details on HOW to craft emails that sell?

That's easily fixed.

Simply scoot here: Email Maverick's Email Playbook.

Frank Zappa

There's no doubt about it. People like to buy stuff.

Why?

The answer is simple.

Cuz people *like* stuff.

However, just because folk like to buy, doesn't mean they'll buy your stuff.

Even if they *want* what you're offering, many times, they *still* won't buy.

You know, I bet you have subscribers on your list right now, who genuinely want what you sell, but are just not pulling the trigger.

What gives?

Here's what:

These subscribers have that ten-letter word starting with the letter: O, that stops them from buying and scares marketers and salespeople senseless.

That word, of course, is: Ochronosis.

You're probably a little confused right now, right?

Well, that's because I'm just messin' with you.

Sorry.

Of course, that ten-letter word starting with the letter "O" is: Objections.

That's right, your subscribers when looking at your sales pages will have objections that stop them from going all the way and buying.

Listen, if you wanna stop your subscribers from abandoning their online shopping carts like a redheaded stepchild, read the following very carefully.

Listen. I want you to take a good hard look at your product or service.

Scratch your brain to come up with a list of objections that might prevent your subscribers from buying.

Some objections might be:

They don't see enough value to pull the trigger.

Maybe they're scared if they buy your product or service that it might not be as good as you say it is.

They may not understand how your product or service works.

Hey, you should go to your sales page and read through it. And after every sales point that you make, stop and say, Hmm, what about what I just said could trigger an objection inside my prospects noggin'. Then go about rewriting it in a way that eliminates that objection.

That's a neat idea, huh?

Hey, if you do this, it can lower your shopping-cart-abandonment rate to a number smaller than Danni DeVito's shoe size.

Hey, why are you just sitting with a stupefied look on your face?

Go and do this little exercise.

Hmm, sometimes I think I want you to succeed more than you do.

Or maybe I didn't communicate the importance of this little exercise clear enough?

Nahh.

It's you.

Babe Ruth

I f (that's a very big 'if') you do email marketing well, every email you send brings a subscriber closer towards a sale.

Maybe I should clarify what doing email marketing 'well' means, eh?

Here's what I mean by doing email marketing well:

It's sending emails that contain the following four elements: (1) Helpful (2) Entertaining (3) Relevant and (4) Have something to buy.

Miss one or more of those four elements and you'll find selling your product or service harder than a book titled *How To Lose Weight And Keep It Off* by Oprah Winfrey.

What?

You think that book might actually sell?

Perhaps you're right.

Ok, Hot Shot, how about this one:

Your product or service will be harder to sell than a book club membership endorsed by Floyd Mayweather.

Ah, forghedaboudit.

Just trust me, you gotta have all four of the above elements in your emails, okay?

"It's never just a game when you're winning."

George Carlin

A h yes, the human species loves to make excuses, don't they? Especially after losing.

Why is this?

The answer is simple.

Losing sucks.

And making excuses such as, "It's just a game," makes us feel better.

Yes, losing in sport can hurt your ego, however, in advertising, it can hurt more than your ego; it can hurt your bank account too.

And in the world of advertising agencies, there is a certain excuse that's thrown around more than Donald Trump's weight. It's an excuse given by ad agencies to their hapless client who can't see an increase in sales.

And the excuse goes something like this:

Oh, yeah, about not getting any immediate sales with the ad campaign . . . Yes, um, what you have to realize is, we are "branding" your business. The ad campaign we created for you is a long-play strategy. In the long run, you'll see the increase, which I can assure you, Mr. Ivan Gottaclue.

What rubbish.

If that's not the lamest excuse for not getting any sales, I'd like to hear it.

Listen: Advertising should only have one objective, and that objective is not to entertain or to create awareness, or to be cute or clever.

No.

The one objective is to make sales!

And, as an email marketer, that should be your *one* objective too.

You know, "branding" has become so vogue in business these days that business owners have foolishly chosen virality and branding over sales.

Listen, Sweetcakes, if you wanna win (make moolah) at email marketing, read the following five words very carefully.

Stop Branding And Start Selling.

Voltaire

H ey, wanna know a secret to making more sales with your email marketing?

You really wanna know?

Oka, I'll tell you.

If you want your subscribers to go from subscriber to buyer, then do this:

Serve them.

Did I just see your shoulders drop and hear you sigh?

Yeah, I get it, it's not a very sexy or exciting secret, is it?

But make no mistake, it's a powerful one, nonetheless.

Listen, long gone are the days when sending a promotional email with a few lines of copy and a few links to your product page was enough.

People have been pitched too so badly and so often that they now delete promotional emails quicker than a teenage boy deletes his phone history.

Nowadays, even your promotional emails have to deliver value.

Listen, I'm gonna lay down one of the hard and fast rules I have for email.

Here it is: Serve first, pitch last.

In *my* book, to pitch first is like having a waiter ask you for a tip before you're even seated.

Now look, I'm not saying you have to give away your best stuff for free or work for free, that would be dumb. You're a business, not a charity, I get that, but why can't email marketing be a great service?

Well, it can.

The first step is to just give a *damn.*

Just giving a damn goes a *long* way.

I want you to adopt the attitude of a world-class butler who goes over and above to make his clients feel like kings or queens.

You know, most marketers only see email marketing as a tool to deliver a sales pitch.

I don't.

I see email marketing as a <u>service</u> to my subscribers and customers.

Do I pitch in my emails?

Does Tiger Woods Like Sex?

Of course I do.

But not without delivering unto my subscribers a most excellent email that contains helpful and practical information they want.

Big difference.

I don't know what it is about the internet, but it seems to lower people's IQ by at least 20 points.

It's like common sense and cyberspace mix as well as oil and water.

You see, no salesperson in their right mind would sit down with a prospect and blurt out a hard-hitting sales pitch without a little small talk, a little conversation to break the ice followed up by some helpful information.

So why do online marketers do that with their emails?

Well, like I said, my friend, because people lose all common sense when doing business online, especially selling via email.

The bottom line is this: Make even your promotional emails super valuable to your prospects. Make it worth their time to read. You know, the best form of selling is serving.

Serve your way to profits, my friend.

Serve, serve, serve.

Deliver, deliver, deliver.

Pour it on, pour it on, pour it on.

Not only will serving your subscribers make you a great business person, but it will also make you a great deal of moolah to boot (especially if you do email the email marketing maverick's way).

"But, when you have to resort to turntables, trick lights, flashing lights, fire and all that, you're actually saying, I need this because what I do is not all that together."

Buddy Rich

Hear this:

When email marketers focus on design over the actual content, you're essentially saying your sales pitch is not all that together, so you (subconsciously) take the subscriber's focus off your weak pitch, and put it onto pretty images and graphics.

Look, unless a salesman walks in wearing nothing but his underwear and his socks, I don't really care *how* he looks.

What I *am* interested in is this: Is he honest? Is he trustworthy? Will his product do for me what he says it will?

How he *looks* is pretty much irrelevant to me in the sales process. In fact, if a salesperson looks too slick, it's almost off-putting and can make you a little suspicious. Better to not draw attention to your appearance at all.

Every good salesperson knows that ALL focus should be on the actual sales pitch. Anything else is just a distraction.

Hear this: You're not trying to win an award in design, you are trying to make a sale. So do away with all those dumb HTML images and graphs. They're only distracting your subscribers from the one thing that matters in email marketing—your sales pitch (the content).

Oh but Kelvin, it makes my emails look so professional.

Rubbish.

They make your emails look spammy and salesy.

If you wanna make more sales, you'll take my advice on this.

But I guess, spammy marketers gonna spam, right?

Hey, can you tell I don't think much of using images?

You have no idea.

"To be persuasive we must be believable; to be believable we must be credible; to be credible we must be truthful."

Edward R. Murrow

N othing boosts credibility like being honest.
Listen:

You may write persuasive and even believable emails; however, if your subscribers don't trust you, they ain't buyin.

You know, back in the day, it was lawyers and car salesmen that were labeled as dishonest and sleazy.

Today, that mantle goes to the email marketer, and for good reason too.

It seems to me that most email marketers today have attended the Lance Armstrong School of Ethics.

They'll do just about anything to get a sale. And if you thought Lance Armstrong could peddle fast and furious, you should see an email marketer peddle their wares to their poor unsuspecting subscribers.

Where to find an honest email marketer?

Well, you'd probably have more luck finding a feminist dining at a Hooters restaurant.

Okay, okay, maybe I'm being a little too hard on email marketers here. Yes, you're right, there *are* some very honest email marketers out there.

And they are the ones who will prosper in the long run.

So what am I trying to say here?

Forgive me. I'm having trouble staying focused Today. What I'm trying to say is this:

Yes, by all means, learn to write persuasive and believable sales copy, however, all that doesn't amount to a hill of beans if you aren't completely honest with your subscribers.

I know I'm preaching to the choir here, but let me say this:

A lot of good honest marketers aren't showing their subscribers that.

How do you show your subscribers your honesty?

Well, do you think telling your subscribers that your product has some flaws would increase your credibility in your subscriber's eyes?

How about not exaggerating your claims and promises?

How about admitting to mistakes?

How about always delivering on what you promise?

How about actually doing what you said you were going to do?

Yes, if you keep displaying your honesty, your credibility will continually grow like the bank account of Bill Cosby's lawyer.

*"I like to get in among a set of people
and get to know them very well."*

J.K. Rowling

I want you to read the following quote (it's from Eugene Schwartz's book *Breakthrough Advertising*) at least ten times.

I'm serious.

In fact, I want you to write it out in your own handwriting and stick it on your bathroom mirror, or on your fridge, or somewhere else where you will see it often.

Why?

Because if you do not learn the sales and marketing truth this quote reveals, you'll forever be as frustrated as a guy with OCD who works at a doorknob factory, and as broke as a strip club owner in Salt Lake City.

Alrighty, here's the quote:

> *"The power, the force, the overwhelming urge
> to own that makes advertising work, comes from
> the market itself, and not from the sales copy.
> Copy cannot create desire for a product. It can only
> take the hopes, fears and desires that already exist
> in the hearts of millions of people, and focus those
> already existing desires onto a particular product.
> This is the copywriter's task: Not to create this mass
> desire – but to channel and direct it."*
>
> ~ Eugene Schwartz

Now let that percolate around in your noggin'.

If you truly understand what was said in that quote, your life as a marketer will become immensely easier.

But alas, a market's mass desire is a complete mystery to most email marketers.

These clueless marketers need to take a leaf out of Mrs. Rowling's book (excuse the pun) and get down from their Email Ivory towers and get in among their subscribers to really get to know them.

Once you *know* your market's common burning desire, well, directing that desire onto your product or service becomes as easy as directing a turd down a toilet.

Sorry.

That last simile was a little crass, even by my standards.

Huh?

You say you thought it was kinda funny?

Really?

You surprise me.

Maybe I don't know you as well as I thought.

"We have learned the lesson that the music industry didn't learn: give people what they want, when they want it, in the form they want it in, at a reasonable price, and they'll more likely pay for it rather than steal it."

Kevin Spacey

W ell, Mr.Spacey, it isn't only the music industry that didn't learn that lesson.

When it comes to getting people to buy, most email marketers are about as competent as Mike Tyson is at investing money.

Listen, that Kevin Spacey quote you just read is probably the best description of sales and marketing I've ever heard.

I'm serious about that too.

And this guy's not even in sales and marketing. He's an actor!

If email marketers were even half as clued-up as Kevin Spacey on what causes someone to buy, they would be very wealthy individuals.

You know, what Kevin Spacey said is what I like to call the "Sales Trifecta."

What is the sales trifecta?

The sales trifecta is simply this:

(1) Have a product or service your subscribers <u>want.</u>

(2) Have it in the <u>form</u> they want it.

(3) Sell it at a price they think is <u>reasonable.</u>

Then, and only then, sweet tender sales you will make.

Easier said than done?

You betcha.

But if you focus on those three elements, it's only a matter of time before your sales will start flowing like lies from the lips of a politician.

That's it for today.

Hey . . .

. . . Keep on keepin' on.

Ozzy Osbourne

F or us online marketers, there are a ton of ways to promote your product or service, aren't there?

Now, keeping with the music theme, let's take a look at five major marketing mediums wherein you can promote your wares.

There is Facebook ads, YouTube, Twitter, Google ads, and Email.

Here's how I would categorize these mediums—musically speaking:

Facebook ads are Country, YouTube is Pop, Twitter is Funk, Google ads are Classical, and Email is Rock.

How is Email like Rock music?

I'm glad you asked.

Here's how:

Email's gritty.

It's got an edge to it.

It's got attitude.

And best of all, Email doesn't demand perfection.

Of all the marketing mediums out there, Email would have to be the most forgiving of them all.

You see, if you screw up your promotion on the other mediums, it will cost you dearly in time and money.

But if you screw up a promotional email?

No worries.

You simply write another, and push send.

Also with Email, you don't have Zuckerberg and his henchmen, or Larry and his pal Sergey (owners of Google) telling you what you can and can't say in your promotions.

Email is your stage, and you can say whatever the hell you wanna say. Yup, email is the perfect medium for imperfect marketers.

You know, I've tried all the other marketing mediums and I tell ya, I felt more censored than Elvis Presley on the Dan Sullivan show.

Trust me, email truly is the Rock God of the marketing mediums, and I know whereof I speak.

Oh yeah, baby, email rocks my world.

Geez, that was a cheesy way to end, wasn't it?

"I just want someone to talk to, and
a little of that human touch."

Bruce Springsteen

If there's one thing that's lacking in most email marketer's emails, it would be this:

Human touch.

And just like the lyrics to Springsteen's song ("I just want someone to talk to"), so do your subscribers.

So be the one they can talk to.

Know this:

Your subscribers subscribed to YOUR newsletter to get help with a certain problem they have.

They're looking to you for information and guidance.

So, give it to them.

Be that go-to-guy (or gal) for your subscribers.

But for crying out loud, do it with some human-touch!

Email marketers get so caught up in their email open rates, click-throughs, and making sales that they forget there's a real human at the other end.

And the net result?

Cold, vapid, and lifeless emails.

Not gonna cut it, my friend.

You ever shake someone's hand, and their hand is so cold and limp it feels like a dead fish?

Well, it's the same feeling your subscribers will get if you send cold, limp emails.

So make damn sure your emails are warm and personable, OK?

Hey, before I finish here . . . gimme an internet high-five, eh?

Ah, c'mon, Pookie.

On three, OK?

Ready? 1,2,3 GO!

Ah, forget it.

Why do I even bother?

Well, it's because I care.

Albeit, a little less now.

"I know a man who gave up smoking, drinking, sex and rich food. He was healthy right up to the day he killed himself."

Johnny Carson

Hmm, kinda reminds me of most email marketers. They don't use stories. They don't have an opinion. They're scared to offend. They don't use humor. They have no original thoughts. They don't dare stray from (the almost sacred) email marketing best practices in fear of (gasp!) the unknown.

They don't write what they *want* to write, the write what they think they *should* write.

In other words, these marketers are such a bore they make Warren Buffet look a charismatic rebel.

Listen, if you're doing email marketing, why not at least make it fun?

Trust me, if you're not having fun writing emails, no one's having fun reading them!

Nuff said.

*"Some can handle it, and some can't. I'm
not interested in the ones who can't."*

Gordon Ramsay

I call my subscribers names.

I use excessive slang.

My similes are, as one miserable Amazon reviewer described them:
Cringe-worthy.

I have turned self-aggrandizement into an art form.

I tell it like it is, and I sure as hell don't pander to political
correctness.

And the subscribers that can't handle it?

Simple.

They unsubscribe.

But listen.

You ever been to a party where there was a small group of miserable
killjoys who put a wet blanket on the whole thing? They sit there
and make other people feel quilty for getting their groove on, but
when they finally get up and leave, the rest of the party rejoices, and
the party takes off.

Well, that's how I feel about my unsubscribers.

They are the party poopers.

I'm glad to see 'em go.

And truth be told, they were never gonna buy a damn thing anyway.
And if they did, you can bet dollars to donuts they'd be a pain in the
culo customer.

And, I'm not gonna lie, a get a lot of unsubscribes.

But, I also get a LOT of fans, too.

Listen, you wanna get yourself some haters.

Why?

Because when you get yourself some haters, you'll also get die-hard fans.

And it's the die-hard fans who not only become your best customers, but they also become your best promoters.

Listen, trying to please everyone in your emails is to please nobody. And let me tell you, there are a lot of email marketers out there pleasing nobody. These vanilla marketer's end up having a list full of subscribers who are indifferent.

They're neither hot nor cold.

These subscribers are as useless as an all-you-can-eat buffet at a runway model convention.

Yup, subscribers who are indifferent are the worst subscribers of all.

They're the "wet blanket" at a party.

But if you follow my Maverick ways, you'll find these subscribers won't hang around very long.

In fact, they'll leave quicker than Donald Trump can say, "Tremendous."

So, what is the Maverick way?

Glad you asked.

Here it is:

Stand for something.

Have one message to one select group and NEVER stray.

Care ONLY for your market.

Be yourself warts and all.

Do things the way you wanna do them.

And if someone doesn't like it . . .

. . . WHO CARES?!

"I tell you, we are here on Earth to fart around, and don't let anybody tell you different."

Kurt Vonnegut

L ighten up . . .
Folk are already uptight . . . don't add to it.

"Rhythm is everything in boxing."

Sugar Ray Robinson

W ell, guess what?

Writing has rhythm too.

Know this:

When your subscribers read your emails, they can sense the rhythm of your writing because they hear the words in their head.

And, if your writing has the rhythm of an all-white Baptist dance party, reader engagement will drop faster than a bad face-lift.

However, if your writing has the rhythm of Miami hip-hop dance club, reader engagement will skyrocket.

How do you know if your writing has good rhythm?

I knew you were gonna ask me that.

It's rather quite elementary, my dear Watson.

What you do is read your copy aloud.

If you stumble over any spots, change it until you can read it without any verbal bottlenecks or stumbles.

Chances are if you're stumbling over a section, so will your readers.

Listen. You want your copy to flow.

But let me issue you a warning.

Don't make it flow so smoothly that you put your reader in a daze.

Remember, this is email marketing, right?

Hear this: I want to keep my subscribers on their toes. I want them fully engaged and ready to take action on my offers.

How do you keep them alert?

Well, we can achieve this changing up the flow of our copy.

For example, if I have just given my reader two big paragraphs, I'm going to make the third one super short.

If I really wanna wake them up, I use a one-word sentence.

So listen up and listen good (that had good rhythm).

Next time you write a promotional email, stop and take notice of your use of the following:

Syllables, punctuation, sentence length, and your hard and soft sounds.

Why?

Because they determine the rhythm of your copy.

Look, if you really want to improve the rhythm of your writing, listen to rap music. I'm serious.

Check these lines by Missy Elliot, and tell me they don't roll off your tongue nicely.

Check 'em out:

> *"I've got a cute face*
> *Chubby waist*
> *Thick legs n shape*
> *Rump shaking both ways*
> *Make you do a double take*
> *Plan rocker show stopper*
> *Flo fropper head knocker*
> *Beat staller tail dropper*
> *Do ma thing motherf#c*kers*
> *Ma Rolls Royce Lamborghini*
> *Blue madina always beaming*
> *Rag top chrome pipes*
> *Blue lights outta sight."*

Not a fan of rap?

No matter.

Because the one writer I consider to be the supreme master of writing with rhythm is a man called Theodore Geisel.

Theo wrote several of the most popular children's books of all time. He sold over 600 million books that were also translated into more than 20 languages

Of course, I'm talking about the author of the Dr. Seuss books.

Here's some of the master's work:

You have brains in your head.
You have feet in your shoes.
You can steer yourself in any direction you choose.
You're on your own.
And you know what you know.
You are the guy who'll decide where to go.

~ Dr. Seuss

Did I ever tell you about the young Zode,
Who came to two signs at the fork in the road?
One said to Place One, and the other, Place Two.
So the Zode had to make up his mind what to do.
Well . . . the Zode scratched his head, and his chin and his
pants.

~ Dr. Seuss

It's a pleasure to read, isn't it?

I mean, you can really feel the rhythm. But if you think it's only kids who like to read content that has rhythm, you are making a huge mistake.

Alrighty, I'm now going to sign off on this little writing lesson with one more great piece of writing.

Here it is:

Little shoeshine boy never get slowed down.
But he's got the dirtiest job in town, bendin' low at the
peoples' feet on the windy corner of a dirty street.
Well, I asked him while he shined my shoes, how'd he keep
from gettin' the blues.

He grinned as he raised his little head, popped a shoeshine
rag and then he said:
Hey, get rhythm when you get the blues.
C'mon get rhythm, when you get the blues. A jumpy rhythm
makes you feel so fine, it'll shake all the troubles from your
worried mind.

That was from the song 'Get Rhythm' by Johnny Cash.

Cool, huh?

Hey Kelvin, this was a great lesson. It also had style, elegance, and humor.

Well . . .

. . . Rat-a-tat-tat, I'm all about that!

"Find the good. It's all around you. Find it, showcase it, and you'll start believing in it."

Jesse Owens

N ow if that's not the exact blueprint of email marketing, I don't know what is.

Yes indeedy, in every email, you should be showcasing your product or service's good points like Kim Kardashian showcases her patootie.

If you truly want your subscribers to believe that your product or service is worth buying, you'd better start showing your product's good points in every email.

Copywriters call these good points: Benefits—not to be confused with features.

Now, I'm gonna break down the difference between a feature and a benefit for you.

Huh?

You say you know the difference? You say this stuff is too basic?

Listen, Buttercup, do you think Roger Federer stops practicing his tennis serve because he thinks he's "got it down?"

Not a chance.

He keeps practicing the same basic serve, time and time and time again.

And so it is with marketing fundamentals.

You should never stop going over them.

Rebuke finished.

Onward.

I'm gonna use a Rolex watch to illustrate the difference between a feature and a benefit, Ok?

Ok.

Check it out:

A **feature** of a Rolex watch could be that it has an 18kt yellow gold band.

A benefit of that feature could be that this allows you to embellish the band with precious gems such as diamonds.

You follow?

Good.

In other words, the **feature** is a fact about the product or service, and the **benefit** is what that fact will *do* for the buyer.

Benefits come from the features.

Now, the benefit I used in that example would really compel a would-be Rolex watch owner to buy, don't you think?

Nope.

It wouldn't.

Am I trying to be a smart ass here?

No, not this time.

What I *am* trying to do here, is get you to fully comprehend the importance of writing benefits of your product or service that are compelling.

You see, having an 18kt gold band that allows you to embellish it with diamonds is a good benefit, sure. But it sure as hell isn't a *compelling* benefit.

And therein lies the reason why so many email marketers struggle to make sales. It's because their 'product benefits' are about as weak as a malnourished kitten with one kidney.

Not good.

Here's a simple fact: Subscribers won't shell out their hard-earned if you only give them *good* reasons. No. Subscribers will *only* hand over their green stuff if you give them *compelling* reasons to do so.

Capisce?

Good.

Alrighty, enough corn. Let me throw you some red meat.

I'm now going to show you, most wonderfully, how to write compelling benefits for your product or service that will cause wallets to open and will also . . .

. . . Drag In Big Fat Glorious Wads Of Greenery!

Ok, ya ready?

Then why are you sitting so far back?

Come in closer.

That's better.

Alright, my little marketing crony, this is how you write compelling benefits.

You simply dig deeper.

By that, I mean this: You ask yourself this question. "What is the benefit of that benefit?"

For example, let's refer back to the Rolex watch.

Remember the benefit of the Rolex watch?

That's right; the benefit was that because the band was yellow gold, it could be further embellished by adding precious gems to it.

Now, what could be a benefit of that?

Hmm, let's see. How about this:

The benefit of having a band that can be embellished with gems could be that you will stand out amongst others as being someone of high status, and you'll be perceived as someone who has achieved success.

But wait.

We are not done yet.

Let's dig even deeper.

What could be the benefit of that benefit?

The benefit of people seeing you as successful could be that you instantly become more desirable to the opposite sex or potential business partners.

You could expand upon this benefit by saying how much more influential and persuasive you will be when others perceive you as successful (because you wear a stunning Rolex).

Do you see how much more compelling your benefits can be when you keep digging deeper?

Well, be sure to apply this digging deeper method next time you sell your subscribers on your product or service's benefits.

"I was dating a transvestite, and my mother said,
'Marry him, you'll double your wardrobe'."

Joan Rivers

I t's true; women are all about their wardrobes, aren't they?

Well, guess what?

Email marketers are all about their email statistics. They obsess over them.

They check their stats more frequently than a teenage girl checks her Instagram, Snapchat, and Facebook accounts combined.

In fact, I'm pretty sure email marketing is a leading cause of OCD.

And do you know which stat email marketers obsess over the most?

Did you say open rates?

Correctamundo.

Well, I'm going to give you a little trick that will almost guarantee your open rates double.

Sounds too good to be true?

Sounds like I'm just writing hyperbole?

I ain't.

Here's the little trick (it's not really a trick):

You ready for it?

You sure?

OKAY.

Drum roll

Write better emails!

"Men want sex and success.
Women want everything."

Gene Simmons

M en are simple.
If you just draw everything back to sex and success, you pretty much have a sale.

Women are more complex.

No one really knows what women want; not even women.

But this you can sure of—selling to women, you will have to hit on many more benefits than just sex and success.

Just something to think about.

Johnnie Cochran

An email marketer is just like a defense attorney—he must have a strong opening line.

Write one too long, you fail.

Write one too boring, you fail.

Want some tips for starting your emails?

You do?

Okay.

Here are some suggestions that are sure to get your subscribers engaged and reading:

(1) Make your opening line short and snappy. One word sentences are best if you can swing it.

(2) Tell the subscriber what you're gonna tell them (i.e., what's in it for them).

(3) Make an *attention-getting* statement using any of the following elements; humor, controversy, contrarianism, weird or wacky, or a little-known fact. Then tie it into whatever it is you're selling.

(4) Make a statement that reflects your subscriber's common thoughts or beliefs (a.k.a. enter the conversation going on in their mind).

(5) Ask a question. This one almost forces them to engage. I use this one a lot.

Look, there are no rules here.

But one thing your opening must achieve is driving enough interest and attention to get them to read on.

It must have an impact.

Your opening line should have the effect of walking up behind someone and pinching them on the arse.

A little crude?

Maybe, but damn it, that is what is needed.

Do you think your subscribers are sitting there all day waiting for your email?

Do you think they start reading your email with their undivided attention and nothing else vying for it?

I rest my case.

Gee, thanks, Kelvin, this is very helpful information.

You're welcome.

"Ah, good taste! What a dreadful thing!
Taste is the enemy of creativeness."

Pablo Picasso

H olla.

Do you know why most email marketers struggle to come up with email content ideas?

You don't, do you?

Well, that's ok, Chief, because I do.

And I'm going to tell you why most email marketers struggle to come up with content ideas.

Rarely is it because they are downright dummies. No. The real problem is that most email marketers are more focused on email best-practices, or as Picasso puts it, "good taste."

And the net result?

The become a copy instead of an original.

You know, if these folks grew a backbone and stopped second-guessing themselves, and would write whatever comes to mind, they would be far more creative.

Listen, the very essence of creativity is to come up with original ideas. And the way to write emails that are original is to approach email marketing the way you want to do it, and not giving a kangaroo's scrotum about best practices or worrying about how other marketers are doing it.

That's right, just being yourself is the most creative and original thing you can do.

Think about it; there's only one of YOU out of 7 billion people.

You are unique.

Your perspective is unique.

Your life experience is unique.

Your voice is unique, unless . . .

. . . you pander to "good taste."

Screw good taste and be yourself.

Now, of course, feel free to follow best practices and copy other marketer's email methodology, but know this:

Your emails will come out being about as original as Melania Trump's convention speech.

I don't recommend it, Bubba.

Yup, Pablo Picasso was right; pandering to Good taste, industry practices, or accepted norms will crush, and inevitably kill your creativity like Aretha Franklin stepping on an ant.

So, if you wanna be more creative, screw convention and do it your way.

Hey, Kelvin, if I adopted this approach to email marketing I would end up being some kind of "Maverick."

Exactly.

Now you're on the trolley!

"You can take an average singer and make them a superstar if the song is great. However, if the song is average, it won't matter how great the singer, it won't be a hit."

Quincy Jones

How does that quote apply to email marketing? Here's how:

You can take an average writer, and they can make a ton of sales if what they are promoting is what the list of subscribers wants. However, if the subscribers don't really want what's being offered, the world's greatest copywriter couldn't sell it.

In the music industry, it's all about the song.

In the email marketing business, it's all about your offer.

Never forget it.

Anyway, that's the eight-ball corner pocket.

"I specialize in murders of quiet, domestic interest."

Agatha Christie

O ne of the biggest insights on marketing I have ever got is this: Marketing is hard.

But you know what?

There is a way to make marketing your product or service infinitely easier.

How?

Look at the above quote. (That quote was supposed to be the clue.)

Hmm, something tells me you probably don't read much crime fiction, huh?

Sorry, that was rather rude of me, wasn't it?

Okay, let me tell you the answer, my dear Watson.

One way to make marketing your product or service a lot easier is to *specialize*.

You know, Agatha Christie was a very creative writer who could have written in any genre. And in the beginning, she did.

But it didn't take Agatha long before she found her niche—crime fiction.

Crime fiction is still fairly broad though.

You've got: Historical mystery, hard-boiled, police procedural, forensic, legal thriller, spy novel, psychological, and on it goes.

'Tis a broad genre indeed. But this little broad didn't bother trying to get her books in *all* those other smaller niches. Oh no, Agatha knew her specialty and her audience, and she never left her lane.

While other authors went broad, Agatha went narrow.

She specialized in domestic detective fiction and ignored everything else. And you could say this narrow or 'going deep' approach worked out pretty good for Agatha Christie.

Yup, this ol' girl became the bestselling novelist of all time. Her novels have sold over two billion copies, and some experts say Agatha is third in the rankings of the world's most widely published books, behind only Shakespeare's works and the Bible.

Hot diggity!

Okay, so let's bring this all back to your favorite topic . . . YOU!

How can YOU become more of a specialist and not be so broad, generic, or general?

Huh, huh, HUH?

Alrighty, let's say you're a fitness trainer. How could you carve out a niche and become known for something specific?

Well, maybe you have come to notice that the majority of your clients are soccer moms. Well, I would highly recommend you become known for being THE fitness trainer to soccer moms.

I would suggest you start marketing to ONLY soccer moms and forget the rest.

Start by changing your business name to something like The Yummy Mummy Fitness Workout, or Cross Fit For Bad-Ass Moms.

Those names could definitely be improved, but you get the idea, right?

Now, one bonus of specializing or becoming known as a specialist is this:

You can charge more.

People simply trust specialists more. Being a specialist implies depth of knowledge and expertise. And people will happily pay extra for that.

You know, when it comes to the medical profession, a general practitioner earns some good coin, no doubt.

But compared to their highly paid colleagues who are specialists, well, the GP is getting paid minor league money while the specialist gets paid major league money.

So, you should take a leaf out of Agatha's novel and specialize.

But of course, you can always just stay broad, general, boring, vague, generic, and have your marketing leave your prospects with more questions than an Agatha Christie's whodunnit plot.

It's up to you Jack (of all trades).

I say specialize.

"Me jumpin' up and down?
I'd blacken both my eyes!"

Dolly Parton

H ere's another Dolly Parton quote that's too good to leave out: *"It costs a lot of money to look this cheap!"*

Ahh, I love that ol' girl.

She's got a personality that's about as big as her bra size, eh?

You know, Dolly doesn't take herself or life too seriously.

And guess what?

That is an excellent attitude to have when writing promotional emails, too.

Stop and read some promotional emails that you get sent on a regular basis, and notice how serious these marketers take themselves. Their emails are as serious as cancer.

For crying out loud, lighten up!

Listen. Just because you're promoting something doesn't mean you have to put your serious pants on.

Just be yourself and be cool. You know, when you stop taking this email marketing thing so seriously, something interesting happens. Here's what that interesting thing is:

Your subscribers start taking you more seriously. That's right! You become someone they want to buy from.

Try it and see for yourself.

*"A special effect is a tool, a means of
telling a story. A special effect without
a story is a pretty boring thing."*

George Lucas

E mail is a tool—a means of telling a story.
An email without a story is a pretty boring thing.

But alas, most marketers do not tell stories.

And that is why they fail.

Yes, a marketer's strength flows from storytelling. But beware of the dark side.

Insincere, boring, vapid and irrelevant; the dark side of storytelling are they.

Easily they flow, quick to join you in a fight. If once you start down the dark path, forever it will dominate your marketing, consume you it will, as it does most marketing morons.

Storytelling you must have my young padawan.

"My aim is to put down on paper what I see and what I feel in the best and simplest way."

Ernest Hemingway

B est writing tip from one of the best writers, right there, my friend.

Now listen: Don't get all nervous about writing. If you can speak, you can write, okay?

You see, essentially, writing and speaking are one and the same— they both deliver a message.

Yes, it's fine and dandy to be a technically good writer, but I've read a ton from so-called professional writers who write such incoherent babble it makes your brain hurt.

It's the same with speakers. So what if you can throw around elegant phrases and you have the vocabulary of a Harvard English professor, if nobody knows what the hell you're talking about, in my prideful opinion, you're a lousy speaker.

Listen, at the end of the day it's all just communication.

And the hallmark of good communication is clarity.

The only question should be: Did the reader (or listener) understand what I just communicated?

Forget style, technique, and all that stuff. That will develop naturally over time.

Focus on clarity.

Focus on clarity like Kanye West focuses on himself. Become obsessed with clarity. Write in the clearest and simplest way possible.

That philosophy kinda helped Hemingway out with his writing, don't you think?

Heed the advice, and you'll become a shockingly good writer, or should I say, communicator.

Yes, aim to be a good communicator, not a good writer. If you do, you'll become a good writer.

Capisce?

"The most important aspect of my personality, as far as determining my success goes, has been my questioning conventional wisdom, doubting the experts, and questioning authority. While that can be very painful in relationships with your parents and teachers, it's enormously useful in life."

Larry Ellison

H mm . . . and very useful in email marketing too, Mr. Ellison. Ah, where to start with this one?

You know, when biz folks look to improve their email marketing, they will obsess over everything from what email marketing provider to use, down to the most granular of details such as how many characters should my subject lines have.

They'll seek out information on everything except for the one thing that really matters, and that is this:

How to write emails that bring in more business.

Look . . .

. . . if you can't write emails that bring in the bucks, then worrying about what email provider to use, what time you should send your emails, or any other minor details (and they are minor), then you're just wasting your time and dime.

I don't know about you, but the reason I do email marketing is to increase my business profits.

Sorry, Sweetcakes, but I don't write these emails to you cuz I like you.

As much as we like to pretend that we are pen pals, we are not.

You open my emails for the sole reason of sucking me dry of all my sales and marketing knowledge to increase YOUR biz profits.

And if I didn't send you emails for the sole purpose of getting you to buy my products, I'd be highly offended by your selfish attitude.

But we're both cool with our little arrangement (aren't we?), because you and I both realize we are doing business.

Anyway, I'm getting more off track than Gary Busey after a few drinks.

Where was I?

Oh yeah, I was saying how folk focus on email marketing minutiae, instead of what really matters—writing emails that bring in boatloads of new business.

But really, who can blame small biz owners for this.

Have you ever typed into Google, keywords such as, email marketing tips, strategies, or best practices?

Well, if you did, what you would see is a lot of articles pop up from so-called email marketing experts pontificating on things such as:

Email frequency, send times, HTML optimizing (how to make your emails more pretty), and, get a load of this one: "The inverted pyramid method." Can you believe this dribble?

Here's what else you'll see—a ton of articles on the "how-tos" of email marketing from the big email marketing software providers.

You know, going to one of the big email marketing providers to learn how to do email marketing is like going to a golf manufacturer and asking the staff there how to improve your golf game.

Look, if you're already rockin' and a-rollin' with your email marketing (making consistent sales) and you wanna geek out on all this analytical masturbation that so-called email experts love to natter on about, then by all means, knock yourself out.

But serious marketers don't give too much attention to the aforementioned list of topics the experts and email marketing authorities love to yap about.

Personally, I pay them no mind.

You see, there are only 3 things you need to improve to increase your email marketing results (more sales), and these three things are:

(1) The quality of your leads.

(2) Your offer.

(3) Your email copy.

Improve them—improve your sales.

Simple.

"Respect the person who gives you honesty, because most will just tell you what they think you want to hear."

Young Buck

Wanna know how to gain the trust and respect of your subscribers?

It's very simple.

Tell the truth.

Does your product or service have a downside or a flaw? Did you screw up?

Then confess these things to your subscribers.

Not only will the truth set you free, as they say, but you'll gain the most important thing from your subscribers you can ever get—their respect.

That's right, nothing gains someone's trust and respect more than admitting your failures.

Your subscribers ain't no dummies.

They know there's no such thing as the perfect product or service, and marketers who claim theirs are, are like the used car salesmen who paint over the rust and says the car's body is in mint condition.

Here's something interesting:

Recently I heard an interview with Robert Cialdini, the author of *The Psychology of Influence and Persuasion*. Cialdini mentioned he was a shareholder of Berkshire and Hathaway and that he receives Warren Buffet's monthly newsletter that is sent to all Berkshire and Hathaway shareholders.

Well anyway, here's the interesting part:

Cialdini mentioned that Warren often starts his newsletters by stating a weakness or a drawback.

150

Cialdini says that not only does Warren study finance, but he also studies persuasion like a fiend. It's no accident that Warren starts with the negative before stating the positive. Warren understands the importance of pre-suasion, says Cialdini.

What's pre-suasion?

It's simply this:

It's getting your reader (audience) into a frame of mind that makes them more receptive to your main message.

In other words, it's the setup for the punchline.

You see, for a joke to be funny, it needs a proper setup.

And guess what?

If you want your product or service claims to be believed, you will also need a good setup.

And the very best setup for a reader to believe a promise or claim is first to state a weakness or a draw back.

You see, when you confess a negative, the reader thinks, "Hmm, this guys being straight with me." Admitting a weakness is very disarming, and it promotes trustworthiness.

Try this in your emails, and I think you'll be shocked at how effective this is.

And you know what? Being honest truly is the best policy.

Hey, I thought it would be a good idea to sign off this little lesson by admitting to one of my weakness.

However, after much thinking, I will not be admitting any weakness to you.

Why?

Because I couldn't think of any.

"I wasn't real quick, and I wasn't real strong. Some guys will just take off and it's like, whoa. So I beat them with my mind and my fundamentals."

Larry Bird

I often read magazines or non-fiction books and get an extreme case of writer's envy.

Their poetic writing, their vast vocabularies make me feel more inadequate than a Ford Fiesta driver pulling up next to a Lamborghini Aventador.

But what I later learned is this:

All that stuff is secondary.

Sure, it's nice if you can write like a Hemingway or an Ian Fleming, but style is small and easily eaten potatoes compared to the fundamentals of good writing.

What are the fundamentals of good writing?

These:

(1) Having something to say worth reading.

(2) Writing with clarity.

Here's what I suggest you do: Forget about trying to be a good writer. Just focus on achieving those two fundamentals.

If you can do just those two things, you'll be light-years ahead of any other writer.

Now, let's focus all this on email marketing.

Listen: You don't have to be a better writer to beat your competition (other email marketers in your industry). However, you do need to write more interesting and easier to read emails.

You know, Larry Bird is a classic example of winning with a superior execution of the fundamentals. Bird was slow, awkward, and moved around the court like an Irishman at the end of St Patrick's day celebrations. Yet, he dominated the sport by mastering the fundamentals.

And guess what?

It's how one dominates any field of endeavor.

Listen:

If you wanna be a winner, you'd better grow to love the fundamentals.

It ain't the easy way, but it's the winner's way.

"Have you seen U2's live show?
It's boring as hell.
It's like watching CNN."

Sharon Osbourne

C ouldn't agree more, Mrs. Osbourne.
     Ah, I love that ol' girl.

Yup, U2 has more money than God, and this affords them such luxuries as . . . well, whatever the hell they want.

When U2 go on tour, they employ more people than all the McDonald's franchises combined.

And when they do live shows, no expense is spared.

They use stadium speakers the size of shopping malls, video screens that make IMAX Screens look like iPod screens, and use more lights and fireworks than Singapore's National Day celebrations.

They turn stadiums all over the world into their very own spacecraft or portable cathedral.

Does all this flash and pizazz make for a better rock concert?

I think not.

To me, all that flash and imagery is just beautiful nonsense.

And Sharon and I are not the only ones who think this.

Here's a quote from a review in The Washington Post: "U2's performance was more of an orgy of light and sound than a rock concert."

To me, a U2 concert is a classic case of image over substance.

The music takes second place to all the special effects. It's like any blockbuster movie getting spewed out of Hollywood nowadays. It's all special effects and very little plot and character development.

What are these Hollywood movie produces thinking?

154

They aren't.

If they are, they can only be thinking this:

Hey, who needs a good story or plot when we can use all these amazing special effects?

But it ain't just movie producers and music artists who are fall prey to image over substance.

Email marketers are even more obsessed with image.

That's right; they want all the bells and whistles. They use HTML, images, fancy fonts, beautiful color schemes, fancy logos and on and on it goes.

How pitiful.

To think any of that stuff will make your emails more effective is stupid on a plate.

All that stuff does is distract your subscribers.

Look, if you want to send your subscribers to a website (via a link in the email) that has images and a product catalog or whatever, fine, but don't cram all that junk into your emails.

Listen:

There is no more effective email than just plain text.

Just words on a screen selling them on whatever action it is you want them to take.

That's all you need, and that's what works.

I know most marketers who read this will disagree.

That's fine.

I love my competition pursuing fruitless endeavors.

"Don't think about the start of the race, think about the ending."

Usain Bolt

B efore you put pen to paper or fingers to keyboard, think on these:

What is the one big idea I want my subscribers to walk away with?

What action do I want my subscribers to take?

What is the emotion I want them to feel once they've read my email?

You know, I've found that the more I focus on the end result, the easier it is to start an email.

The End.

*"When a man is on the right path,
he must persevere."*

P.T. Barnum

T hey say a person needs to be exposed to a product or service at least seven times before they consider buying.

I don't know if that's true or not, but what I do know is this:

In general, people need a helluva lot more exposure than what you think.

Selling is a process.

Before a subscriber buys from you, they must first trust you, and trust is built over time.

Getting your subscribers to know, like and trust you is the goal, but you'd better be prepared to send a lot of emails.

But alas, when it comes to email marketing, most business owners have the perseverance of a man attempting to solve the Rubik's Cube who's color blind and has ADHD.

Listen, all the business owners who quit email marketing too soon are losing business to those business owners who never quit.

Email marketing is like knowledge—a little is a dangerous thing.

Okay, Kelvin, so how long should I keep sending emails to my subscribers?

That's a great question. However, you're not gonna like my answer.

Here's my answer:

Until they buy or die!

Told you.

*"There's no alcoholic in the world
who wants to be told what to do."*

Anthony Kiedis

I recently read Anthony's autobiography and lemme tell ya, it's one heck of a read.

Kiedis reveals stuff in that book that would make Charlie Sheen blush.

I highly recommend it if you're into rock biographies.

Well anyway, in one of the chapters, Anthony talks about his rehab experience and how impressed he was with the program.

Anthony says the genius of the program is that they realize you can't preach sobriety or try to make converts out of alcoholics. Thus, they make it a program of attraction, rather than a program of promotion.

You see, if they can get the addicts to see someone who has made a great recovery, then some of the addicts will see that and think, "That guy used to throw up on his trousers, now he looks like he's enjoying himself."

But the minute you say, "Hey, this is what you should be doing," to an alcoholic or a drug addict, nothing will come of it. There's no addict in the world who wants to be told what to do, says Kiedis.

Well, guess what?

The same holds true for email marketing.

No subscriber in the world wants to be told what to buy. The minute you tell a subscriber what they should buy, nothing will come of it.

However, if you vividly show a subscriber what your product can do for them, they'll start to imagine themselves having that result in their life.

In other words, give them a vision to buy into.

As the late, great negotiation expert Jim Camp (a.k.a. the world's most feared negotiator) was fond of saying, "Vision precedes decision."

You see, when you give someone a vision of what they can have, instead of telling them what they should buy, they feel like they are making the decision to buy all by themselves instead of being sold to by some pushy marketer.

Harken: The art of the sale is to get someone to buy and have them think they sold themselves.

Know this:

People love to buy, but they hate to be sold.

Okay, to sum up:

Don't tell your subscribers what they should buy, instead, show them visions of what your product or service can do for them.

Paint vivid pictures.

Get your subscribers using your product or service in their mind's eye.

Give them a vision so they can make a decision, okay?

Don't write emails of promotion . . . write emails of attraction.

Here endeth the lesson.

"It requires a certain kind of mind to see the beauty in a hamburger bun."

Ray Kroc

When Ray Kroc first saw one of the McDonald brother's hamburgers, he didn't just see a hamburger; he saw a business empire.

That's right. He was able to see past the actual hamburger.

Listen: When it comes to email marketing, if you can't see past the actual writing of emails, you should quit now.

In other words, if you can't see the enormous potential to boost your business's bottom line, you do not see the forest for the trees.

Know this:

You can take a hamburger bun and make some serious bucks, and you can write an email and make some serious bucks.

The only question is:

Can you see the beauty in an email?

*"My best pick-up line is,
'My name is Hugh Hefner.'"*

Hugh Hefner

L et's talk about subject lines.

People place far too much importance on subject lines.

Subject lines are more overrated than Jerry Seinfeld. C'mon, if you really think about it, he's not really that funny, is he?

Whatever.

Now, hear ye this:

If you do email marketing properly, meaning, you write entertaining, relevant, and helpful emails, your subject lines become increasingly less important.

In fact, your subject lines will become totally irrelevant.

You see, if you keep sending your subscribers emails they love to read, they'll start opening ALL your emails. At this point, they are barely reading your subject lines. They see an email from YOU, and they open.

So I contend that the sender's name is way more important than the subject line.

I guess you could say it this way:

Your best subject line should be your name!

That said, writing damn good subject lines should still be the goal.

The truth is, as I mentioned earlier, the *sender name* IS more important than the *subject line*.

However, it takes time to build your 'name' to the point where your subscriber's open your emails just cuz it's from YOU. Credibility and rapport must first be established.

And a key factor in building this rapport and credibility with your subscribers early on is getting your emails opened in the first place. Thus, at the beginning (before you've established your name), your subject lines are extremely important.

Make sense?

Timothy Leary

L isten up Buttercup . . .

. . . Marketers who seek to make sales also lack ambition.

Look, I don't wanna make sales, I wanna make customers.

Not any old customers, either.

No siree! I want good-hearted, good-humored buyers who become lifetime customers.

You know, the difference between a lifetime customer and a one-off sale is the difference between an apple and an apple tree.

One will feed you for a day, the other, a lifetime!

How do you grow a list of lifetime customers?

Same way you grow an apple tree, Bubba. With a little (not too much) tender love and care.

Do it right, and you'll have a money tree before you know it. Oh yeah, and don't forget to prune your list regularly too, you know, to get rid of the "bad apples."

Anyway, the root cause of all this chasing after one-off sales comes down to a lack of ambition.

Listen, start thinking long-term when it comes to your sales.

Think bigger—think lifetime customers.

*"Humor is the great thing, the saving thing.
The minute it crops up, all our irritations and resentments
slip away and a sunny spirit takes their place."*

Mark Twain

L isten up:

If you wanna become a master salesperson, you'd better get good at making your subscribers feel good.

Know this: Your subscribers all have some crisis going on in their lives.

Sometimes they're wound tighter than a two-dollar watch.

But if you can write promotional emails that put a smile on their dial, well, you've gone a long way towards making the sale my friend.

Don't ever underestimate the power of humor.

The more you can get your subscribers to smile (or at least smirk), the more they will grow to like you.

And in sales, if your prospect likes you, the sale is already half done.

"If you want to build a ship, don't drum up the men and women to gather wood, divide the work, and give orders. Instead, teach them to yearn for the vast and endless sea."

Antoine de Saint-Exupèry

H ear this:

If you wanna motivate subscribers to buy your product or service . . .

. . . then stop going on and on and on and on and on and on and on and on (too much?) about your product or service and start talking about what your product or service will ultimately do to improve their daily lives.

Create a vision that will inspire action.

Listen:

The omission of a 'vision' causes indecision.

If you, for example, sell a weight loss product, then don't be waxing lyrical about its damn ingredients, instead, create the vision by talking about them being able to run around with their kids with boundless energy because of their new lighter selves.

In other words, sell the result.

Create the vision.

Take the order.

"Ric Flair is the greatest guy ever. He just wants to hang out, have a beer, and tell stories. He's the coolest."

Bill Burr

That quote is my exact sentiments when it comes to email marketing.

My emails aren't designed so much to teach or pitch my wares (truly) as they are to build a relationship with my subscribers.

In my eBook, a great promotional email is one that makes the subscribers feel like their hanging out with a friend over a few beers and tellin' a few yarns.

But, Kelvin, I'm interested in making sales and increasing my business profits, why are you going on about drinking beer and telling stories?

Look, Jimmy. I've just given you the single biggest way to boost your business profits.

That's right, just hanging out, having a few beers and telling stories, metaphorically speaking, *is* the best way to increase your business profits.

It's called 'bonding' with your subscribers, my friend.

Ain't nuttin more powerful.

He that hath an ear to hear this message will prosper.

The rest?

They will continue to be seen as the "pain in the culo" marketer they are.

Which one will you be?

Friend or foe?

"Real success is not on the stage, but off the stage as a human being, and how you get along with your fellow man."

Sammy Davis, Jr.

T he real success of an email marketer is not in their email copy, but in their product or service and how they treat their customers.

At the end of the email, you either have a product or service that truly helps your subscribers, or you don't.

And, you either give a damn about your subscribers, or you don't.

Sure, email copy is important, but compared to having a great product or service and caring for your subscribers, it's small potatoes, entry level, bush league, exiguous, two-bit, small fry.

*"Anybody can jump a motorcycle. The
trouble begins when you try to land it."*

Evel Knievel

A nybody can write a promotional email. The trouble begins
when you try and get them to buy.

True, eh?

"My husband can do the work of two men. Unfortunately, those two men are Laurel and Hardy."

Jo Brand

L et me tell you something about me.

My vocabulary is far superior to that of Ernest Hemingway's.

Ernest Hemingway in his last few days that is.

You see, during the last few years of Hemingway's life, he suffered from depression, psychosis, and bipolar disorder. His mental health was severely deteriorated, and he drank himself into a state of permanent stupor.

Obviously, he was not stringing together too many coherent sentences at the time, let alone writing masterful pieces of literature.

Look, I'm not kidding when I say I have a limited vocabulary.

My vocabulary is as bad as, like, whatever.

Geez, Kelvin, that's too bad considering email marketing involves so much writing. Having a limited vocabulary must really suck?

Not so!

In fact, my limited vocabulary has turned out to be a blessing in disguise.

You see, when it comes to sales copy (promotional emails), big words and flowery sentences (stuffed full of adjectives) hurt your writing, not help it.

They slow a reader down.

George Orwell said: "Never use a big word when a short word will do."

Yep, not only does using short, simple words make your writing easier for your readers, but it makes it easier for you, too.

Mark Twain was a big fan of simple words for that very reason.

Here's what Mr. Twain said: "I never write 'Metropolis' for seven cents because I can get the same price for 'city.' I never write 'policeman' because I can get the same money for 'cop.'"

Listen, it's not that you have to dumb down your writing for your subscribers, it's just that they can't be bothered to work out what the hell it is you're saying. Don't make your reader have to work—they won't.

Make your writing effortless to read.

Avoid using big pompous words so you readers can avoid stubbing their eyeballs.

Your copy should flow like the rants out of Mel Gibson's lips.

You know, I would love to take great pride in the fact that my emails contain no big fancy words.

But I can't.

Because like I said earlier, I couldn't write emails with big fancy words if I wanted to.

"There's not a single muscle on my body that doesn't have a purpose. Because I'm not a do nothing b*tch."

Ronda Rousey

V erily I say unto you . . .

There's not a single product or service feature/benefit that can't be turned into a promotional email.

There's not a single fear or desire of your market that can't be turned into a promotional email.

There's not a single event (no matter how exciting or boring) in your life that can't be turned into a promotional email.

Listen, there are not 101 content ideas for selling your product or service.

No.

There is an infinity of content ideas for selling your product or service.

Huh?

You say that's pure hyperbole?

Listen, Buckwheat; you obviously don't know this little trick for coming up with email content ideas.

The trick?

Hmm, I don't feel like telling you now. I mean, I'm just a serial exaggerator, right?

Oh look, maybe I'm being a little too sensitive.

OK, here's the trick (formula):

You take **x and tie it to Y.**

X being: Any topic, theme, object, person, place, animal, concept, event (a.k.a your idea), and **Y** being: Your product or service.

Here's an example.

Let's make X a banana and Y a financial planning business.

Then what you do is, you tie the two (X and Y) together.

How?

Simple.

You find a point of similarity between a banana and financial planning.

Hmm, let's see now.

Ah, I've got it.

How about this: A banana and financial investing both have small windows of opportunity.

That can be our tie-in, ok?

The email could go something like this:

Bananas have a really small window of opportunity to be eaten, don't they?

Most folks think all is lost with a rotten banana. But they are very wrong.

I used to chuck out rotten bananas, too, but here's what I do now:

I put them in the freezer, and then, later on, I put them in the blender and make a banana milkshake.

The flavor is unbelievably good.

Why am I, a financial planner going on about bananas?

Well, let me tell you.

You see, a lot of folks over 60 years of age who have not yet started investing money for their retirement are just like folks when their bananas go rotten—they think all is lost.

But, that doesn't have to be the case.

Not at all.

You see, just like I turned my rotten banana into an enjoyable milkshake, these latecomers to the investment table can turn their situation into an enjoyable retirement by making some simple (but very effective) strategic financial decisions.

If you feel like you've come late to the financial investing table, here are four things you can do right now . . . yadda yadda yadda . . .

See there?

I just promoted a *professional service* using a freakin' banana!

The way I see it, there's no reason ever to say that you don't have any email content ideas.

Not ever.

Am I saying that you're a do-nothing b*tch if you say you can't think of content ideas for your emails?

YES.

That's exactly what I'm sayin'.

"If I can get you to laugh with me, you like me better, which makes you more open to my ideas. And if I can persuade you laugh at a particular point I make, by laughing at it you acknowledge its truth."

John Cleese

I don't think I can add anything to that insightful quote. So, I won't.

    . . . But seriously, chew over that quote.

John Cleese

T he marketer who makes his subscribers laugh most *earns* best.

 Make no mistake, my friend, the email marketer who can make their subscribers laugh, has a huge advantage over the other 99% of email marketers who don't. You know, it seems to me the most common strategy for selling in email nowadays is to bore their subscribers into buying their product or service.

Now listen:

I'm not just flappin' my jabs when I say humor helps an email marketer.

Studies have shown that humor enhances retention, and relieves stress and anxiety.

Not only does humor enhance learning and retention, but it makes you more likable.

And any savvy salesperson knows that if they can get their prospect to like them, the sale's half made.

Research on likability dates back to the 1960's. And surprise, surprise, humor is always found to be leading quality people desire to have, and admire in others.

Psychologist Norman Anderson (a leading expert in likability) states that a sense of humor is a major factor in determining how likable someone is.

Look, the bottom line is simple:

If you wanna make hay with email, develop your sense of humor.

Can you develop your sense of humor?

Yes, of course.

Huh?

You want to know how?

Simple.

Watch comedians and read funny content.

It's what I do.

You know, I have developed my sense of humor to such a high degree that sometimes my own jokes go over my head.

"The main thing a musician would want to do is to give a picture to the listener of the many wonderful things he knows of and senses in the universe."

John Coltrane

T he main thing an email marketer would want to do is to give a picture to the subscriber of the many wonderful things his product or service will do for them.

Know this:

In sales, vision precedes decision.

A subscriber will only become a customer if they can see in their mind's eye, how much better their life will be with your product or service in it.

But alas, most business owner's emails create about as much vision as a broken TV in a blackout.

They focus far too much on general information. They have a ton of facts and features and helpful tidbits. Now that's all well and good, but it ain't enough to make someone buy.

You see, people buy emotionally. And the language of emotion is imagery.

You want to focus more on creating emotional imagery than on putting forth a logical case on why they should buy your product or service.

Don't tell them about how much your product will help them . . .

. . . SHOW THEM!

The bare bottom line is this:

Use less logic in your pitches and create more vision.

Speak to your subscriber's emotions.

You know, most email marketers are so left-brained (logic biased) they walk with a slight slant to the left.

Trust me, sales is a right-brained business.

But how do you go about creating a vision for your subscribers? Is there a system, a methodology, or a type of mind map to follow?

Look at you . . . that was the most left-brained question I've ever heard.

Listen, don't over think this.

Creating a vision for someone is as simple as doing the following:

Tell stories.

Stories about customers who have had success with your product or service.

Use more visual language. Use your words to paint pictures in your subscriber's minds.

And cuz I'm feelin' extra generous today, here's one more tip.

After you have written a promotional email, read through the entire email and ask yourself: Did any images pop into your mind? What did your mind's eye see? If no images popped into your mind, that means your words did not paint any pictures for your readers to imagine.

If no images came to mind, what then?

Please tell me, Lieutenant, you didn't really ask that question.

I'm out.

Paul Hogan

L isten: If Paul Hogan made crocodiles the main focus of his movie (Crocodile Dundee), he would not have had nearly as much success. In fact, I would hazard a guess the movie would have been a complete flop.

You know, as much as you may think folk are interested in crocodiles, they are nowhere near as interested in them as they are people.

The same holds true for email.

As much as you think your subscribers are interested in your product or service, they are nowhere near as interested in it than a good character-driven story.

Not knowing this is an email marketer's biggest point of weakness.

Yup, we all love a good character-driven story.

The Email Marketing Maverick's way of selling is about people; it's 10% about the product or service.

That's right, 90% of my emails are about people.

I write character-driven emails.

When selling your wares, your emails should be 90% about your prospect and 10% about the product or service.

If you want your emails to be a struggling independent documentary, focus your promotional emails on your product or service. (That's not an email.)

If you want your emails to be a blockbuster movie, you will focus your promotional emails on character-driven stories. (THAT'S an email!)

"We are all in the gutter,
but some of us are looking at the stars."

Oscar Wilde

Y our subscribers have a problem.

They see your product or service as a solution.

They subscribe to your newsletter.

Now what?

Well, you've gotta make 'em see the stars, Lars.

I shall explain:

Your subscribers, regarding their problem, feel like they're in the gutter. They are looking for your product or service to get them out.

So I submit to you that your product or service is the stars.

And every email you send your subscribers should open their eyes to see another sparkling benefit your product or service can bring them.

And if you can make your product or service shine brighter than your competitors, your product becomes the Dog Star (the brightest star in the Earth's night sky), and your competitors appear as faint specs in the background.

Then what?

Well, those who have eyes to see will buy.

Those who don't, won't.

Simple.

Oh yeah, and those subscribers who opt-in to your list just to grab your free stuff . . .

. . . You should drop your pants and give 'em the moon.

Flea (Red Hot Chili Peppers)

G reat musicians don't just play.
And they don't just study.

They do both.

When they're not playing, they're studying, and when they're not studying, they're playing.

And that is what makes them great.

How does this apply to email marketing?

Here's how:

Great email marketers also play and study.

A great email marketer is a real player. (i.e. They're always growing their email list, and they're always sending emails to that list.)

And like a great musician, when they're not playing, they're studying.

And guess what they study?

What's that?

You say they study the classic marketing and sales books?

I'm sure they do, but that's not what makes them great.

No, I'm talking about something else they study that truly separates them from the rest.

So guess again, Bubba.

Ah, forget it.

I'll just tell you.

They study Quantitative Methods in Economics.

Nah, I'm just screwin' with ya.

No, what they study is this:

Their Market!

Yes, siree.

Listen:

For a musician to succeed, they need to know what to play.

For an email marketer to succeed, they need to know what to say.

Yup, a musician who doesn't know the song will play all the wrong chords.

Not good.

And a marketer who doesn't truly know his market will say things that don't strike a chord with his market.

Geez, I milked that analogy completely dry, eh?

Look, the point is this:

You gotta play AND study.

But study your market more than you study anything else.

If you do, you'll find selling your product or service to your subscribers will become as easy as playing the radio.

And . . .

. . . You'll start makin' more sales than the RHCP's drug dealer.

"I've never lost a game. I just ran out of time."

Michael Jordan

L et's talk about the reasons why people don't buy.

There are many reasons why a subscriber doesn't buy what you're selling them.

But I think you can boil them all down to four main reasons:

(1) They don't want it.

(2) They want it but can't afford it.

(3) They're not convinced your product or service will deliver what you say it will deliver.

(4) They're a tightwad. Yup, in the words of Oscar Wilde, "Some people know the price of everything and the value of nothing."

Oh, I do despise those good for nothing penny pinchers.

OK, now let's look at the buyer.

Who is the buyer?

The buyer is a subscriber who wants what you're offering, has the wherewithal to purchase it, and does.

Now hear this:

The secret to email marketing is all about building a list that has more buyers than it does people who fall into the four categories above.

Hey, did you like the Michael Jordan quote?

It's a great mindset to have.

And BTW, I've NEVER lost a sale. I just take a while to close the deal sometimes.

"Society questions the police and their methods and the police say, 'Do you want the criminals off the street or not?'"

Kurt Russell

S ometimes a subscriber will question me and my methods. I used to have a pat answer.

That pat answer was this:

"Get lost!"

That's right. I would show 'em the unsubscribe button.

But then there were times where I was feeling a little more generous, and so I would tell them this:

"If you have any thoughts and opinions on how I approach email marketing, do please keep them to yourself."

But now . . .

thanks to Mr. Kurt Russell, I have a new response:

"Do you wanna make sales or not?"

You likey?

"To me, music is just entertainment — what else can it be? In fact, it's the only language I know of that's universal."

Ray Charles

T o me, email marketing is just entertainment—what else can it be?

Yeah, yeah . . . it can be information and promotion.

Look, emails can have information and promotion in them, sure, but it is my contention that email marketing IS entertainment.

I know many email marketing exp-hurts would debate me on this.

But guess what?

It's these same exp-hurts who jump on forums and bitch and moan about poor open rates and sales performance.

You know, I've given up trying to convince these marketing PhDs (Please Hire, Desperate) to make their emails more entertaining.

They seem to have a patent on boring emails, and they don't look to be giving that up anytime soon.

To finish off . . .

. . . I've compiled a list of the four most boring things in the world.

Being in a waiting room for hours on end.

Doing your taxes.

Being stuck in traffic.

Reading one of those email marketing exp-hurt's emails.

They are that bad.

"The record business. It is exactly what it is: Record — Business. You have to take care of both, or they won't take care of you."

Dr. Dre

It's no wonder Dr. Dre has a net worth of $740 million.
The guy gets it.

If you wanna make it in the music bidnezz, you can't just make good music, you gotta make good deals too.

Now, let's apply this Dr. Dre street smarts to email marketing.

Email Marketing is exactly what it is: Email and Marketing

If you wanna make it in the email business, you can't just write good promotional emails, you gotta be a good marketer too.

You see, email marketing in the hands of a biz owner who's a savvy marketer will make some serious chedda.

On the flip side, email marketing in the hands of a chump marketer will only make chump change.

You see, to build a big-ass email list you're gonna need to drive a ton of foot traffic to your store or a ton of online traffic to your web page. Or both.

So the message is clear: Don't just focus on writing emails and don't just focus on building your subscriber list.

You gotta take care of both, Homie.

Then, and only then, will they take care of you.

*"It's official, Arnold said he will enter the race for Governor.
At least that's what everybody thinks he said."*

David Letterman

Y ou gotta love Arny, eh?

I mean, this guy can't lose.

Sure, there was that infidelity incident involving his children's nanny. By the way, have you seen her? Sheesh, Arnie's eyesight has definitely deteriorated over the years.

Well anyway, apart from that little indiscretion, this guy's been kicking goals his whole life.

I mean, there's nothing this guy can't do.

As a young man, he decided to become the best bodybuilder in the world.

So he did.

Then he wanted to become the highest paid actor in Hollywood.

So he did.

Then he got a little bored for a moment and decided it would be a good idea to become the Governor of California.

So he did.

What's his secret to success?

Well, there's all the obvious stuff like hard work, patience, and natural talent.

And yes, the guy's likable and charismatic as hell, but if I had to highlight one attribute that makes this man so great, it would be this:

He's a Maverick at heart.

Ah yes, a man after my own heart.

Yup, it's his way, or it's hasta la vista, baby!

Check out the following words from the big man himself:

"You must absolutely ignore the naysayers. All my life I have had people telling me, "Arnold, you are crazy. Nobody has ever done that. It's not possible!" At first, that bothered me, but soon I realzsed that these people meant only that it was not possible for them. Their rules did not apply to me. I was always ready to break the rules; not the law; the rules."

Arnold Schwarzenegger

Words to live by, I say.

I tell ya, breaking the rules (being a Maverick) will truly set you apart.

You'll get noticed while everyone else who's busy dotting their i's, and crossing their t's, and copying each other fade away into oblivion.

You'll start stealing the show.

And in the competitive world of email marketing, you can't afford not to stand out.

Verily I say, if you apply this mindset to your email marketing, it will be your name that stands out in your subscriber's inbox.

That's right. You'll steal the limelight just as Arnold did to Dave Letterman in this message.

"I am like any other man.
All I do is supply a demand."

Al Capone

How well you do with email marketing will come down to two things:

(1) How strong your market's demand is, and (2) how well you supply that demand.

Maybe I can't help you with point #1, but when it comes to point #2 . . .

. . . I'm Your Huckleberry.

If you have a good product or service and a list of qualified subscribers, I'll show you how to turn subscribers into customers like Capone turned Downtown Chicago into his own place of business.

Yes, my little marketing crony, I'll get you writing emails that cause your subscribers to take the action you want them to take, and get them to like doing it.

Whether it's visiting your store, website or buying your product or service, I'll show you how to blatantly pitch your business in every email and . . . have subscribers thank you for it!

You know, it should be illegal to write emails this good.

William Faulkner

T here is no such thing as a bad email.

Some emails just happen to be better than others.

In fact, I would go so far as to say that your bad emails should be celebrated.

Did you send an email that got little to no sales?

Good.

You now know you need to look at your three elements (your list, offer, and copy) and ask yourself, "What da hell?"

Did you write an email that got a pitiful open rate?

Good.

You learned what makes a bad subject line.

Did you send an email that had a strong click-through rate but nobody bought anything.

Great.

You know they're interested in your product or service, but not enough to buy. Now you can get about improving your offer.

But like the late, great Billy Faulkner and I said earlier, "There is no bad."

This is very true with email.

You see, *if* you're writing emails the way I teach (the Maverick's way), even if your response wasn't what you expected, you can be damn sure these three (very good) things still happened:

(1) Your subscribers would have got to know you a little better.

(2) Your subscribers would have learned something valuable. Thus

they will like you that little bit more.

(3) Your subscriber's trust in you will have deepened.

Yep, if you follow my Maverick methodology, then every single email you send will strengthen your relationship with your subscribers.

Not bad, eh?

"Some folks look at me and see a certain swagger,
which in Texas is called 'walking.'"

George W. Bush

S ome folks look at me and see a self-conceited, sneering egomaniac, which in business is called 'marketing.'

Listen:

If you can't sell yourself, how the hell are you supposed to sell your product or service?

Most business folks are so self-effacing they make Tom Hanks look like Kanye West.

Look. I like humble people, and humility is certainly a character trait everyone should cultivate. However, in the world of promotion and advertising (email marketing), being humble will send you to the poor house quicker than Harrison Ford can say "no" to an interview.

Sure, be a humble individual, but when you're promoting yourself and your business . . .

. . . You Best Get To Braggin'!

"This whole thing called the internet, and all this other kind of stuff is about to go crazy. It's all going to change. But, you know what's not going to change? The talented people."

Jamie Foxx

I n the entertainment industry, it's the most talented performers who make it big.

In the business world, I submit to you that it is the most talented salespeople who make it big.

Think about it.

As a salesperson . . .

You have to sell yourself on the idea that you can make it in business.

You have to sell others on working for you.

You have to sell your loved ones on supporting you in your business venture.

You have to sell your market on the idea that your product or service is the right choice for them.

That's a lotta selling, Bubba.

Now listen:

It's true that the internet has brought with it many opportunities for the average business owner. However, as the great Winston Churchill wisely put it: *"With great opportunity comes great responsibility."*

And for those of us who are blessed enough to have this 'great opportunity' (living in a country with a free market and access to technology), what is our responsibility?

I believe it is this:

To Master The Art of Selling!

You owe it yourself, your loved ones, your business, your employees and yes, your community.

Your level of success will come down to your ability to sell.

You see, if you boil business down to its core, it is this: The act of buying and selling goods and services.

But guess what?

Everyone wants to buy, but nobody wants to sell.

I get it. Buying stuff is fun.

But Listen. If you learn to love *selling* as much as you love *buying*, eventually you will become a master salesperson.

And by virtue of that, you will be able to buy all the stuff your greedy little heart desires.

William H. Bonnie (Billy The Kid)

T hat quote is simply an older (and cooler) version of: "Don't count your eggs before they hatch."

Now hear this:

I always hear other email marketers babbling on about their open rates, click-through rates like they mean something.

They obsess over these two metrics like Rain Man over a fallen box of toothpicks.

Listen, the only thing really worth tracking and obsessing over is this:

Actual Sales!

You see, you can write a promotional email that gets a tremendous open rate and a smokin' good click-through rate and still not make a red cent.

Getting a subscriber to open your email, click on your link, but not buy, is the digital version of: "Thanks, I'll get back to you." And any experienced salesperson knows what that means.

Listen, open rates will not feed your kids.

Click-throughs will not pay the bills.

Sales are what matter.

Sales are what count at the start of the day, the middle of the day, and the end of the day—every day.

The only metric you should obsessively track is your units sold.

As the late business guru, Peter Druker was fond of saying: "What gets measured gets improved."

*"Life has become immeasurably better since I've
been forced to stop taking it so seriously."*

Hunter S. Thompson

nd so will your emails if you stop taking them so seriously.

"I would rather write 10,000 notes
than a single letter of the alphabet."

Beethoven

I'd rather write 10,000 promotional emails than make a single cold call.

Just sayin'.

Sonny Liston

L isten up, Champ,
The greatest sales technique you can ever use is *proof.*

Without proof, all your product or service claims don't amount to a hill of beans.

Nope.

People want (and need) proof.

Listen, your subscribers want to believe you, but they've been lied to and cheated on more times than Tiger's wife, and they're now as skeptical as hell.

So what is an email marketer to do?

That's easy.

You give them the proof they need.

In all your emails, you should be displaying your expertise. That's right, you should be giving them real actionable and honest to God advice. Demonstrate your knowledge within your emails. Are your subscribers trying to lose weight? Then give them tips and help them understand how weight is lost and gained. Tell stories about the folks you have already helped to lose weight.

You follow?

*"I like to have a peek, see what the audience is
doing during the opening act, because it gives
you a clue and gives you a good feeling of where
you are — the air can be different in different places."*

Mick Jagger

A wise performer will tailor their performance to fit their audience.

A comedian knows if he tells a redneck joke in a Nashville club, it'll go over like a turd in a punch bowl.

He also knows if he tells a redneck joke in a New York club, he'll get laughs.

It's all about knowing your audience.

In marketing, we call that your 'message to market match.'

I know, I know, it can be tricky to get a good read on your market with email marketing. I mean, you can't see these people. They're just a list of names on a database. With email marketing, you can't just peek behind the curtain to get a good 'feel' for your audience, right?

Wrong!

You most certainly can, Bubba.

Here's how I go about getting a good feel for my subscribers (audience).

Every once in a while, I like to scan through my database of customers and subscribers. What I'm doing is, I'm looking for clues that will tell me who these people are.

You'll be surprised how much intel a simple email address can give you.

What am I looking for?

I'm looking to see where my customers live. I'm looking to see if they are male or female (sounds creepy, doesn't it?). I'm looking to see what industry they're in. You know, a lot of email addresses will flat-out tell you the subscriber's name and business name.

Priceless.

Okay, what else can you do to get a good feel for your audience?

Well, every once in a while, I like to invite my subscribers to hit reply to my emails. You know, communicating with my subscribers has given me a ton of invaluable information on how to better serve them. I don't have to guess what they need help with . . . they tell me!

Of course, you have to give them a good reason to do so.

You see, your subscribers are like teenagers. You almost have to trick them into having a conversation with you, but if you can get them talking, you'll both end up having a great chat.

Look, I think you're picking up what I'm putting down here, right?

Just to be sure, what I'm saying here is this:

Get more hands-on with your subscribers!

Yes indeedy, when it comes to your subscriber base, you need to be more hands-on than Donald Trump with a female civil servant.

End of lesson.

"Education is the kindling of a flame,
not the filling of a vessel."

Socrates

T hat quote holds very true for selling.

Listen: 'Selling' is taking a prospect's already existing desire that your product or service fulfills, and intensifying it, and channeling it right onto your product or service.

Know this: We do not create our prospect's desire any more than the inventor of the solar panel creates the sunlight.

But just like the inventor of the solar panel can harness the sun's light and channel it into cells that convert the light into energy that will power his entire house, we too can harness our prospect's desire and channel it onto our product or service that will convert into sales.

Hear this:

No marketer has ever filled a male prospect with the desire to be someone of high status and importance, yet many a marketer has shown a male prospect how their product will make them someone of high importance and high status.

End of lesson.

"Facebook just sounds like a drag, in my day seeing pictures of people's vacations was considered a punishment."

Betty White

I f I had a dollar for every time a lazy slob business owner has told me they don't have time to write promotional emails, I would not be writing this right now.

No. I'd be sipping Margaritas on the beach.

Listen, if you are struggling to find the time to write promotional emails for your business, I hereby give you a solution:

Get off the damn Facebook.

And stay off!

"People should focus more on basic form, the shoulder line and balance, which no one talks about, and study board shaping and wave and wind patterns."

Kelly Slater

I hear ya Kelly.

And I'll tell you why surfers don't talk about those things.

It's because those things aren't cool or sexy.

It's the same reason why email marketers never talk about market research, direct marketing, and copywriting.

Yup, surfers wanna focus on and talk about cool tricks and maneuvers like 360's, aerials, and kick-flips.

And email marketers wanna wax lyrical about ninja tricks and tactics. They obsess over things like the latest and greatest email templates, the coolest "NLP subject lines" and click-through rates.

All of which means a big fat nothing if you haven't first grounded your righteous-self in the fundamentals.

Take a look at anyone who's at the absolute top of their game. I don't care what industry or field of endeavor. I'll bet you dollars to donuts the people at the very top have mastered the fundamentals. You may see only the flash and the highlights now, but the reason they can produce these amazing results is that they are more entrenched in the fundamentals than Chris Christie in a hammock.

That's right, the best of the best have learned to sweep aside all the glitter, the gloss, the glamour, the sexy, and the shiny and instead, they have dug down deep into the unglamorous, bland, and unexciting fundamentals.

Except to them, they aren't dull and boring.

Ohh no. They love the fundamentals like sharks love blood.

Hey, do you remember the movie *The Karate Kid* where Mr. Miyagi tried to teach Daniel the fundamentals of form and movement by getting Daniel to wash his car, sand his floor, and paint his fence?

And do you remember how Daniel thought he was being exploited and that Mr.Miyagi was full of hot air?

Well, let me tell you something . . . over the last few years, I have come across my fair share of Daniel-sans.

I regularly have people (Daniel-sans) contact me who are full of piss and vinegar about email marketing and who want me to teach them my Maverick ways. However, their enthusiasm quickly disappears when I give them a list of things they should do to improve their email marketing.

Things like study Direct Marketing, study the great copywriters, and major in market research.

Whatever.

The fact remains, all success flows out of mastering the fundamentals.

Trying to succeed in anything without first mastering the fundamentals is like building a house upon the sand—even if you can build something that resembles a house, it sure as hell won't last.

"As soon as somebody farts around me, I think it's hilarious. This is something my brothers did that now the boys at work are obsessed with. You cup it, and then you throw it in someone's face and say, 'Take a bite out of that cheeseburger!'"

Jennifer Lawrence

K elvin, you can't possibly come up with an email marketing lesson from that quote!

You're right.

I can't.

To be honest, I threw in that quote for my daughter Brooklyn who is a huge fan of Jennifer. (Love you, Chookie)

Sorry.

Next.

"I try to catch them right on the tip of his nose because,
I try to punch the bone into the brain."

Mike Tyson

T he difference between the *great* athletes and the *good* athletes often comes down to killer instinct.

I'm talking about that quality in a team or individual that drives them to pull out all the stops and go hell for leather (could I use any more clichés?) no matter how exhausted they may be.

In the dying minutes of a game, when the game is hanging in the balance (yes I can!), it will be the team or individual who possesses this killer instinct that will end up the victor.

And it's no different in the email game.

It's the email marketer who will send that extra follow up email, put that extra benefit into the sales copy, write that outrageous subject line, or rewrite their email for absolute clarity that will prevail.

In other words, it's the email marketer who will do whatever it takes (within the bounds of good taste and legality) to get their product into the hands of their subscribers who will win the sale!

Listen to this little ditty, if you will:

The loser <u>tries</u> email marketing.

The hack <u>wants</u> their email marketing to be profitable.

The winner <u>makes</u> their email marketing profitable.

But of course, the winner has that fire that smolders deep inside their soul.

It's called killer instinct baby!

You either got it, or you don't.

"Pleasure in the job puts perfection in the work."

Aristotle

I f writing promotional emails is like pulling hen's teeth for you, then you're doing it wrong.

By that I mean, you're taking it too seriously.

Most promotional emails nowadays have all the charm and cheer of a suicide note.

For crying out loud, stop taking your business, yourself, and your life so seriously.

You're not writing *a will* here . . . you're writing to people who want to know more about your product or service.

You know, most business owners are so uptight that if you shoved a lump of coal up their butt while they were writing an promotional email (that would be difficult, but if you could), by the time they finished, you'd have a diamond. (Tip of the hat to *Ferris Bueller's Day Off.*)

Look, I get it, the struggle is real.

Writing can be tedious as hell.

And that's why you need to heed this advice:

First and foremost, write to entertain YOURSELF.

Yes, I'm saying you need to see if you can amuse yourself with your emails. Write something that makes YOU feel inspired, or laugh, or just engaged.

Listen, as sure as dog crap smells, if you're bored while writing your emails, your subscribers will be bored reading them.

Alrighty, I'll finish with this:

Sometimes all you need to do to get better results with something is to just change your attitude towards that something.

As a wise man once said, sometimes when you care less, you perform better . . . Oh, wait, that was me.

*"All I need to make a comedy is a park,
a policeman, and a pretty girl."*

Charlie Chaplin

I love Email.

All you need to make money with her is a computer with internet access, an email account, and something to sell.

She's beautiful in her simplicity.

And deadly in her efficiency.

Hey, Kelvin, what about direct mail, or Facebook ads, or Pinterest, or Google Adwords, or Twitter?

You can have 'em.

I'll take my Sancha Email Marketing over the rest of those *glamour* mediums any day of the week.

Sure, Email might not be the most sophisticated or prettiest girl at the bar, but she puts out like no other.

Sorry.

I apologize for this metaphor.

But it clearly illustrates my point, doesn't it?

Whatever.

"Doesn't matter if the glass is half-empty or half-full. All that matters is that you are the one pouring the water."

Mark Cuban

I 've been fired from every job I've ever had.

I've been blacklisted from several marketing forums.

LinkedIn rejects about 50% of my content.

And just recently, Zuckerberg and his henchmen booted me off Facebook (shut down my ad account).

Growing up, I gave my mother and teachers so much pain in their brain (through my passive aggressive behavior), they gave up on me. Now, don't get me wrong; I was not a bad kid.

In fact, I was one of the nicest and most respectful kids you would ever meet. That's right. I was a rebel with the good manners and values.

Unfortunately, what I valued more than anything else, was this:

Control.

Yup, I wanted (and still want) 100% control of my life.

Thus, my inability to follow the rules and obey those in authority.

But like I said, I was not overtly defiant.

No, what I would do is lull the person in charge (parent, employer, teacher) into a false sense of security.

In other words, I acted as if I was fully intending on following their orders to keep them happy and to not cause a scene. Then, I would simply go off and do my own thing and deal with the consequences later, if need be.

As the saying goes: It's easier to ask for forgiveness than it is permission.

I have found that to be very true.

However, I have also learned (the hard way) that this beautiful logic has screwed up repercussions when advertising your business on someone else's platform, such as the aforementioned sites.

Thus, the Email Marketing Maverick was like a man with no country, until . . . he found a resting place at good ol' Amazon.com.

I must say, Amazon has been good to the Maverick, however, when I stop to think about how little control I actually have over my books on their platform, I become about as nervous at Stephen Hawking near a swimming pool.

You see, on Amazon (or any other behemoth platform), I'm not the one in control. I'm nothing but a peasant begging for my fill. All I can do is hold out my glass and hope Mr. Jeff Bezos pours into it.

Then how do you get 100% control of your marketing?

Enter: Email Marketing.

Ah, yes, email sweet email.

Yep, email is the one marketing platform that truly gives you 100% control of your promotions.

You can sell whatever you want, to whomever you want, whenever you want, and however many times you want.

And, you can do it the way you wanna do it.

You are beholden to no uptight adjudicators, idiot administrators, and self-righteous moderators.

Yes, email allows a dictatorship.

You become a marketing king (or queen), and your subscribers become your subjects.

However, if you do not possess the sales and marketing knowledge to go with all this control and power, your reign as king or queen can be very short lived.

You see, with email, you can't get the bounty by being "salesy."

Nope.

You're gonna have to learn how to, in a sense, sell without selling.

I know that sounds like double talk, but trust me, it ain't.

In other words, you need to know how to write entertaining emails that also entice your subscribers to take the action (buy your stuff) you want them to take and have them enjoy doing it.

If you can do that, you will have a long and prosperous reign indeed.

If you're ready to begin your reign, go hither: Email Playbook.

"Whether you like it or not, learn to love it, because it's the best thing going. Wooooo!"

Ric Flair

T o this day, it still shocks me how many (misguided) business owners undervalue, and underutilize email marketing.

A 5-minute Google search will give you ample data on the ROI on all the marketing mediums.

And if you take the time to do that, guess what you'll discover?

You'll find countless articles all stating this: As far as ROI goes, email beats the pants off every other marketing medium out there.

I defy anyone to provide evidence to the contrary.

Trust me; you'll have more chance of finding Ted Cruz at an anti-gun rally.

Hmm, I guess that's a little too far-fetched, isn't it?

OK, you'd have more chance of finding Bigfoot. That seems more likely, doesn't it?

Now, once you discover email marketing is the best thing going (in terms of bang for your buck), the question is:

Can you learn to love it?

Well, let me ask you this:

If for every dollar you spend on email marketing you got 38 dollars back (that is the DMA's most recent report); could you learn to love email then?

What did you say?

You say you're already convinced about email marketing, but you're not sure how to write profitable emails?

Well geez, why didn't ya speak up earlier?

You would've saved me all that writing.

Oh well, not to worry.

I've got your back, just boogie on over here: **The Maverick's Email Playbook.**

Now listen, I know I'm not everyone's cup of tea. I can be an insufferable jerk at the best of times.

But know this:

Once you start applying the little-known secrets and principles in my Playbook, and you start to see an increase in sales (i.e., more customers to your store, more of your widgets and online products sold, or a drove of more clients), trust me, Bubba . . .

. . . You'll Learn To Love Me!

You can visit Kelvin here – www.kelvindorsey.com

Louis C. K

I'm always yammering on about writing entertaining emails, aren't I?

Why do I keep harping on about this?

Because I believe writing boring promotional emails is the underlying cause of poor open rates, and thus sales.

And guess what?

I believe I have put my finger on the reason WHY biz folks keep farting out boring emails.

Would you like to hear it?

Okay.

The reason business folks keep writing yawn inducing emails is because they think their subscribers are *not of this earth.*

In other words, they think their subscribers are sophisticated professionals who have no sense of humor or selfishness or greed or fear or love or hobbies or secret fantasies or envy or generosity or hate or kindness or curiosity or passion.

Are you picking up what I'm putting down here?

Look, in all seriousness, if you think your subscribers are too sophisticated for fart jokes, you're way off the mark. Not only are you way off the mark, but you're also unnecessarily putting your subscribers on a pedestal.

Listen. I can't tell you how often I hear this:

I can't say that in my emails, or I can't use slang, or I talk about pop culture, or I can't be opinionated.

Listen, Buckwheat. You can't afford NOT to do all those things.

Look, your subscribers are human beings for crying out loud.

You know, they're made out of that stuff called "flesh and blood?"

They're like you, me, and everybody else—dressed up monkeys in a concrete jungle.

Sure, us humans have learned to suppress our primal desires in public, but our primal desires are always bubbling just below the surface looking for any chance to take over the operation.

To think that your subscribers are somehow immune to all those primal desires is ludicrous.

People are people.

CEO's of fortune 500 companies dream of being rock stars.

Brain surgeons read the National Inquirer.

Accountants tell dirty jokes.

Librarians laugh at farts.

Most marketers need to stop trying to be so damn professional and start being real!

But, Kelvin, I like to write my emails in a professional manner and tone.

Listen, I would like to drink beer and eat pizza every night.

But I don't because that would eventually kill me.

But guess what?

If you keep writing your promotional emails in that "professional tone," you're gonna kill your response. You'll struggle to raise an eyebrow let alone a pulse.

Because truth be told, what "professional tone" really means is this:

Communication that's void of all emotion, opinions, and personality.

The bottom line is this:

People are sick and tired of corporate speak.

The marketer who can communicate with passion and personality will win the email marketing game.

End of story

www.kelvindorsey.com

Printed in Great Britain
by Amazon

61173540R00129